GETTING
THINGS
DONE

Also by Edwin C. Bliss:

DOING IT NOW

GETTING

THINGS

DONE

The ABCs of Time Management

Revised and
Updated Edition
for the 1990s

E D W I N C. B L I S S

ILLUSTRATIONS BY MALCOLM HANCOCK

Futura

A Futura Book

This revised edition first published in the United States
in 1991 by Charles Scribner's Sons.
First published in the United Kingdom in 1992
by Futura Publications, a division of
Macdonald & Co (Publishers) Ltd, London & Sydney.
Revised and updated edition
Copyright © 1991 by Edwin C. Bliss
Copyright © 1976 by Edwin C. Bliss

A CIP catalogue record for this book is available from the
British Library.

ISBN 0 7088 5362 5

Printed in Great Britain by Cox & Wyman Ltd,
Reading, Berks.

Futura Publications
A Division of
Macdonald & Co (Publishers) Ltd
165 Great Dover Street
London SE1 4YA

A member of Maxwell Macmillan Publishing Corporation

To Libby,
who practices what I preach

There is nothing which I wish more that you should know, and which fewer people do know, than the true use and value of time. It is in everybody's mouth, but in few people's practice. Every fool, who slatterns away his whole time in nothing, utters, however, some trite commonplace sentence, of which there are millions, to prove, at once, the value and the fleetness of time. The sun-dials all over Europe have some ingenious inscriptions to that effect; so that nobody squanders away their time without hearing and seeing daily how necessary it is to employ well, and how irrecoverable it is if lost.

LORD CHESTERFIELD
Letters to His Son

CONTENTS

Contents

INTRODUCTION TO THE REVISED EDITION

In the years since *Getting Things Done* was first published, I have conducted seminars and training sessions for tens of thousands of people throughout the United States, Canada, and Europe. In working with these people I've been impressed by several things:

- [ ] Everyone seems to have the same problems. Lawyers, engineers, executives, accountants, salespeople, secretaries—all of them have pretty much the same complaints.

- [ ] The answers to their problems are often quite simple. Not easy, but simple. They do involve effort and determination and vigilance, but they aren't complex.

- [ ] The secrets of effectiveness are not secrets at all. They are principles we are all aware of but too often have failed to put into practice. We need to be reminded more than we need to be informed.

- [ ] In analyzing their time problems, people put the blame in the wrong place. They blame their boss, their subordinates, their customers, their competitors, the system, the New York office, the person at the next desk. They should blame themselves.

- [ ] Change is possible. I have a thick file of letters from people who have changed their lives by putting into practice the suggestions contained in this book.* They will work for you, too.

*And if you have any comments, please send them along. My address is 2220 Carolyn Street, Kingsburg, CA 93631.

In preparing this revision I've been gratified to find that extensive changes were not necessary. I've added some things, changed emphasis in a few places, and tidied up a bit, but I haven't found much need to recant. After all, time management isn't a rapidly changing field. It's true, of course, that new technology affects how we do things—modems and e-mail and laptops and cellular phones and online databases are useful tools—but the *principles* of time management are as basic as the laws of physics. So don't be surprised if much of what you read here seems to be the sort of thing Benjamin Franklin would advise. Old Ben was a world-class master of "getting things done," and if he were around today, I think he'd be pleased to find that all of his precepts were IBM-compatible.

INTRODUCTION

I *first became interested* in patterns of time use many years ago when, as an assistant to a United States senator, I was struck with similarities in the operating styles of the more successful members of Congress. Faced with urgent and conflicting demands on their time—for committee work, floor votes, roll calls, speeches, ceremonies, interviews, briefings, correspondence, investigations, constituents' problems, and above all, the need to be informed on a wide range of unrelated subjects—they develop techniques for getting maximum benefit from minimum investments of time. They learn to set priorities in relation to their own goals rather than someone else's; they learn to screen themselves from unwarranted interruptions; they learn to delegate, to plan, to concentrate on important things, and to disregard trivia. If they don't learn, they don't return.

More recently, as a consultant, I have worked with top executives of hundreds of corporations. Again I have been impressed by the way the more successful ones always seem to have ample time for important matters, such as planning, and manage to stave off intrusions and activities that are nonproductive or trivial. It is true that they have more opportunity than most people to delegate time-consuming tasks, but that is only part of the reason for their effectiveness. They think in terms of objectives rather than activities; they make most decisions quickly; they speak and write concisely; they avoid procrastination; they treat their time as the precious and limited resource that it is.

As I became more conscious of time use, I began to apply in my own life some of the techniques I had observed, realizing that I was not one of those favored few to whom effective time use came naturally; and when I found how much more I could accomplish, I decided to write this book. The subjects are listed alphabetically, but if you'd prefer to begin with an overview of what time management is all about, I'd suggest that you start with "Categories of Time Use."

Incidentally, most of the examples used in this book relate to the business world and to the office, but I hope you won't take that to mean that these concepts are useful only in business. The principles of time management are universal, and they apply in any setting. The techniques that can make corporate board meetings more effective are the same techniques that will put life into the meetings of the social committee of a square-dance club.

Before you begin, think for a moment about time. Could you define it? Probably not. The best my American Heritage Dictionary could come up with is "a nonspatial continuum in which events occur in apparently irreversible succession," which I don't find very helpful. I much prefer Ben Franklin's well-known definition: "Time is the stuff of which life is made."

If you will begin thinking of it in those terms, you are already on your way toward some drastic changes in the way you live . . . from this moment on.

HOW TO GET THE
MOST FROM THIS BOOK

Before you begin reading this book I'd like to make two suggestions.

First, read with a red pen or a yellow Hi-liter in your hand, and mark every passage that touches a sensitive nerve, every idea that could make a difference in your life.

Many people do this habitually but don't get much benefit from it because when they finish the book, they put it on a shelf, never to be looked at again, and all of those good intentions are forgotten. Just marking pertinent passages in this kind of book isn't enough. So—

Second, after you've finished the book, take your tape recorder and a blank cassette tape, and go through the book page by page, dictating a note to yourself about every marked passage, indicating how it applies to you. Don't just recount what you're doing wrong, make a commitment and make it with emotion. Don't be self-conscious—nobody is going to hear the tape except you, so talk to yourself like a Dutch uncle. Don't comment on what you "should" do; talk about what you are *going* to do. And be specific. Some examples:

☐ Don't say, "In the future I'm going to pay more attention to my real priorities." That's meaningless. Instead say, "Effective immediately, no matter how busy I may be, I will schedule some prime time every day to work on something in the "Important but Not Urgent" category.

☐ Don't say, "I'm going to stop procrastinating." Instead say, "From now on I will begin each day by tackling the most unpleasant item on my 'To Do' list—before I get involved with my incoming mail."

☐ Don't say, "I'm going to handle paperwork more efficiently." Instead say, "When handling paperwork, my goal is going to be to 'Do it, Delegate it, or Ditch it.'"

When you finish your tape, you will have a valuable possession, a cassette loaded with advice and encouragement from the world's greatest authority on you and your needs! Any time you need a shot in the arm, just drop that tape into your cassette deck as you're driving to work, and when you get there, you'll land running.

Some time ago, following a series of seminars I conducted in England, I received the following letter:

Mr. Bliss:
After attending your seminar in Bristol, I took your advice and made an audiotape that same day, noting how the principles you discussed applied to my particular situation. I play the 15-minute tape en route to work each morning, and find I arrive at work as motivated to put those ideas into practice as I was when I left the conference hall.

If you make such a tape based on this book, it will change your life. That's a promise. Trust me.

GETTING THINGS DONE

After-Action Reports

When *your annual meeting* is over, before you pack up all the unused brochures and settle your account with the catering manager, sit down in a quiet corner and make two lists: (1) everything you did right, and (2) everything you did wrong. Then put it in the file for next year's meeting.

The military calls this an after-action report, and it's one bit of military red tape that is worthwhile and should be adopted by any organization of any size. Such a report should be made on any significant activity that is going to recur in the future, whether it's a convention, a corporate acquisition, or a backpack trip. Memory is treacherous, and a year from now you will have forgotten the valuable lessons you learned this time around.

Your brief written record of what happened and why, including recommendations for how to do it better and more quickly next time, can save a lot of time and energy.

Alcohol

A *drink before (or with)* lunch is a good way to transform early-afternoon prime time into secondary time. Alcohol is a depressant, and if you use it in the middle of the work day, you are diminishing your effectiveness.

But it relaxes you, you say. True. But in midday this kind of relaxation is the last thing you need.

A secondary effect of a drink before lunch is that it sharpens the appetite, causing you to order a heavier lunch than you would otherwise—compounding the problem of afternoon lethargy.

The head of one advertising agency dealt with the problem by calling his staff together and saying, "It has come to my attention that quite a few of you make it a practice to have a three-martini lunch. I want you to know that I have no objection to this—what you do on your lunch hour is your own business—but I would appreciate it if you would have those martinis made with gin rather than vodka. I realize that vodka is a little more difficult to detect on the breath, but that's just the point. When you call on our clients in the afternoon, I'd much rather have them think you're drunk than stupid!"

In recent years the ritual of a cocktail prior to a business lunch has become less common, which is encouraging. The old navy custom of refraining from drinking until the sun is over the yardarm is still a sound policy.

Behavior Modification

Misuse of time seldom involves an isolated incident; it usually is part of a well-established pattern of behavior, and to change for the better we often must grapple with a habit that has been developed over many years.

There are two ways to change behavior patterns. One (described in the section on procrastination) involves forcing yourself to practice the new behavior pattern until it becomes ingrained. The other involves gradually "shaping" behavior through a system of rewards, the behavior modification technique generally associated with B. F. Skinner of Harvard.

If you were to go all the way with behavior mod, you would plot carefully, perhaps on a logarithmic graph, the specific

habits you wanted to reinforce or extinguish so that you could accurately measure your progress. And you might want to try aversion techniques, which cause undesired acts to evoke unpleasant associations.

For most of us, though, the important thing to learn is that *any behavior that is followed by something pleasant tends to be reinforced and is more likely to happen again.* You can get this reinforcement from others, but you can also reinforce your own behavior by giving yourself some kind of token reward for accomplishing (or starting or sticking with) a difficult or tedious task; staying with a priority item instead of getting sidetracked on a secondary job; getting started on an unpleasant task; turning down an unimportant but time-consuming request. The reward can be something trivial, as long as it has pleasant connotations. It can be tangible—a stick of gum, a drink of water, a snack. It could be giving yourself permission to do something—taking a break or leaving work a little early or buying a pair of shoes. Or it can consist of nothing more than giving yourself a mental pat on the back every time you take a small step in the right direction.

An example of how positive reinforcement can alter behavior is a study on smoking reported in the *Journal of Consulting and Clinical Psychology.* [1] Participants had all smoked at least twenty-five cigarettes a day for at least a year and were asked to abstain for at least a month, an accomplishment that was verified by monitoring the carbon monoxide levels in their blood. Those who succeeded had no more support than the others. What made the difference is that they used positive reinforcement, reminding themselves frequently of the health benefits and rewarding themselves with "gifts" purchased from the money they had saved by not buying cigarettes. Those who failed used negative reminders, such as how weak they would seem if they went back to smoking or punishing themselves for slips.

So there are two points to keep in mind: (1) punishing yourself for failure is not nearly as effective as rewarding yourself for success, because positive reinforcement is by far the most effective way of changing behavior; and (2) you must reward yourself for each *small* success, not just for major achievements. If you start working on your income tax but soon get tired and quit, don't punish yourself for your failure; instead, reward yourself for having started the task. Then contrive another token reward to give yourself when you get started again.

Bottlenecks

A *bottleneck* can occur in an organization of any size whenever a key person fails to take an essential action, whether because of indecision, laziness, mistaken priorities, stubbornness, or overwork. It is a time management problem of the greatest magnitude since it wastes the time of an entire group of people.

Typical bottlenecks are caused by the corporation executive who refuses to say yes or no to a new idea; the bureaucrat who demands unnecessary paper work before approving a project; the club social committee that can't decide the details of a dance far enough in advance to give the decoration committee time to do a good job; the boss who delights in finding trivial imperfections in typing and demands that letters be done over; the teacher who waits until the last possible day to assign

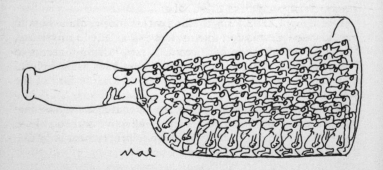

term papers; the boss who insists on being consulted on every decision made by subordinates but frequently isn't available for such consultations. The list is interminable. Most people don't realize how much they thwart the efforts of subordinates and co-workers by failing to respect their time needs.

While a bottleneck can result from a person having too much to do, it can also result from not having enough to do. In that situation many people hoard paperwork, building up a backlog to convince others (and often themselves) that they are busy. Like a tightwad nursing a drink in a night-club, they can diddle with a project indefinitely, giving the impression that something is happening. In such a case the solution is to give them more to do, not less, and set deadlines. This often works amazingly well as a purgative for a clogged pipeline.

If you are a victim of bottlenecks created by your boss or by others in the organization over whom you have no authority, what can you do?

Plenty. You don't have to be a victim. Here are five suggestions:

1. *BE A SQUEAKING WHEEL.*

Remind, hint, beg, cajole, plead, write memos. Stop muttering to yourself and take some action. Keep in mind that to get anything done in this world you must be willing to make a nuisance of yourself if that's what it takes.

One thing that can make this process more palatable is to get advance permission to nag. For example, you might say, "Boss, the deadline for the monthly report always seems to sneak up on us. I know how busy you are—would it be helpful to you if I were to remind you about the twenty-fifth of the month so you can start getting your material together?" Any boss will agree to that, of course, so now you have a mandate to initiate action: "Boss, you wanted me to remind you about the monthly report. Today's the twenty-fifth. Is there anything I can do to help you?"

2. BYPASS THE SYSTEM.

I know of a department head in the San Francisco city government who wanted a partition removed from his office several years ago. The appropriate inspectors came and analyzed the situation, determined that the work would cost $1,500 and would take two weeks to complete. The following Saturday morning the department head and three of his workers removed the partition, repaired and painted where necessary, and finished the job in two hours, at no cost to the taxpayers. They no doubt had broken a few union rules, some safety regulations, and a couple of civil service requirements—but they got the job done.

Remember Hooper's Law:* In a bureaucracy it's always easier to beg forgiveness than to get permission.

3. ANNOUNCE THAT YOU WILL TAKE ACTION "UNLESS . . ."

If you can't conveniently bypass the system but don't want to be stymied by delay, write a memo saying, "Unless I hear from you to the contrary, here is what I plan to do. . . ." This saves time for everyone involved, protects you from repercussions, and enhances your reputation as a "doer."

4. MAKE IT A MATTER OF HONOR.

When someone promises to get a task done by a certain date and you suspect they won't, just ask, "Can I have your word on that?" It's surprising what a difference that simple little query makes. It signals to the other person that you are really serious about the deadline. Having given their word, they have a sense of obligation that they otherwise wouldn't have.

If it's a matter of some importance, write a memo of con-

---

*Named after Rear Admiral Grace Hooper of the U. S. Navy, who established a reputation for cutting through red tape.

firmation. It takes only a few seconds, and a written reminder of the commitment makes a big difference with those who consider verbal agreements nothing more than expressions of intention.

5. *USE POSITIVE REINFORCEMENT.*

On those occasions (and they may be rare) when people *do* get something to you on time, don't take it for granted. Thank them profusely and let them know how much you appreciate their promptness. Lay it on thick. Give them a reputation to live up to. Of all the techniques for changing the behavior of others, this is the most powerful—and the least used.

Breaks

To *work* for long periods without taking a break is not an effective use of time. Energy decreases, boredom sets in, and physical stress and tension accumulate when a person stays with one thing too long. Irritability, chronic fatigue, headache, anxiety, and apathy can all be caused by failure to provide a change of pace during the working day.

A break need not be a "rest" break; indeed, switching to a different kind of work often can provide as much relief from tension as simply relaxing. Switching for a few minutes from a mental task to something physical can provide such a break. Walking around the office or around the block can serve as a quick restorative break. Changing from a sitting position to a standing position for a while can break up the monotony and provide some physical stimulus. Isometric exercises—tensing various muscles and working them against each other—can be done at your desk and are a good way to get a break from work.

Merely resting, however, is often the best course, and you

should not think of a restorative break as poor use of time. Not only will being refreshed increase your efficiency, but relieving tension will benefit your health. Anything that contributes to health is good time management.

Briefcase

> *The first grader asked his mother why Daddy brought home a briefcase full of papers every evening. She explained, "It's because Daddy has so much to do he can't finish at the office and has to work nights." "Well, then," said the child, "why don't they just put him in a slower group?"*

If *you are an* executive, you occasionally will have to take work home with you. That's the price you pay for the perquisites of office. But if you find yourself doing it on a regular basis, it's a sign that something is wrong; either you are trying to do too many things yourself (see "Delegation"), or you have failed to organize your time at work effectively. A third possibility is that you may be suffering from a martyr complex and are trying to impress your associates or your family with how overworked you are (see "Workaholic").

You need to get away from work at the end of the day, both mentally and physically. Except in emergencies, time spent at home in the evenings doing office work tends to be counterproductive, draining your energies and alienating your family. The homework habit can also dampen your drive to get things done at the office because you tell yourself, "If I don't get this finished today, there's always tonight."

It isn't worth it. The only justification for taking your briefcase home every evening is that you intend to use it the following morning for transporting your lunch.

Categories of Time Use

Tasks can be broken down into five categories:

1. Important and Urgent
2. Important but Not Urgent
3. Urgent but Not Important
4. Busy Work
5. Wasted Time.

1. IMPORTANT AND URGENT

These are the tasks that *must* be done immediately or in the near future. Examples: Your boss demands a certain report by 10 A.M. tomorrow. Or your engine blows a gasket. Or the labor pains are three minutes apart. Or it's April 15 and you haven't finished your income tax form.*

Now, unless these situations all develop simultaneously (God forbid!), you can cope with them. Because of their urgency and their importance, they take precedence over everything else, and procrastination is out of the question. It is not here that we find our time management problems.

2. IMPORTANT BUT NOT URGENT

Attention to this category is what divides effective individuals from ineffective ones.

Most of the really important things in our lives are not urgent. They can be done now or later. In many cases they can

---

*This is an example of a task that began in Category 2 and escalated to Category 1 now that you have reached the deadline.

be postponed forever, and in too many cases they are. These are the things we "never get around to."

Examples: that special course you want to take to upgrade your professional skills; that new project you would like to suggest to your boss after you find time to do the preliminary fact-finding; that article you've been meaning to write; that diet you've intended to begin; that annual medical checkup you've planned to get for the past three years; that visit to a lawyer to have your will drawn; that retirement program you've been planning to establish.

All of these tasks have one thing in common: Despite their importance, affecting as they do your health, your wealth, and your family's welfare, they will be postponed indefinitely unless you yourself initiate action. If your activities are keyed to other people's priorities, or to system-imposed deadlines that make things "urgent," you will never get around to your own priorities.

3. URGENT BUT NOT IMPORTANT

In this category are those things that clamor for immediate action but that we would assign a low priority if we examined them objectively.

For example, someone asks you to chair a fund drive or to give a speech or to attend a meeting. You might consider each of these low priority, but someone is standing in front of you waiting for an answer and you accept because you cannot think of a graceful way to decline. Then, because these tasks have built-in time limits, they get done, while Category 2 items get moved to the back burner.

4. BUSY WORK

There are many tasks that are marginally worth doing but are neither urgent nor important. We often do them ahead of more important things because they are *diversionary*—they provide a feeling of activity and accomplishment while giving us an excuse to put off tackling those Category 2 tasks that have a far greater benefit.

One aerospace executive, for example, told me of going to his office the previous Saturday morning to do some work he had been postponing. He decided first to organize the materials on his desk. Having done so, he decided that while he was at it he might as well straighten up the desk drawers. He spent the rest of the morning reorganizing drawers and files.

"I left the office feeling vaguely disappointed that I hadn't accomplished what I went in for," he said, "but I consoled myself with the thought that I had been very busy doing some worthwhile things. I realize now that I was playing games with myself—working on low-priority tasks to give myself an excuse for further delay on the far more essential task I originally had assigned myself."

If you find time constantly being diverted by minutiae, try following the advice in the section on procrastination.

5. WASTED TIME

The definition of wasted time is subjective, of course.

Ernest Hemingway is quoted as having defined "immoral" as "anything you feel bad after." I don't know whether that definition will stand up to theological scrutiny, but I do think it can be applied to wasted time. Television viewing, for example, can be time well spent if we come away feeling that we have been enlightened or entertained. But if afterward we feel that the time would have been better spent mowing the lawn or playing tennis or reading a good book, then we can chalk up that time as wasted.*

People who scramble madly to get control of their time often look in vain for things in this category upon which to

---

*By any sane person's standards, about 95 percent of all television viewing must be put in this category, which is something to think about the next time you reach for that remote control.

blame their inefficiency. I am convinced, however, that with most people this is not where the problem lies. It lies rather with allocating too much time to things in Categories 3 and 4 rather than to those in Category 2.

Cellular Phone

Whenever I am asked my opinion of the cellular phone, I am reminded of the response of Circuit Judge N. S. Sweat, Jr., of Corinth, Mississippi, when asked about whiskey. He said:

> If when you say whiskey you mean the devil's brew, the poison scourge, the bloody monster, that defiles innocence, dethrones reason, destroys the home, creates misery and poverty, yea, literally takes the bread from the mouths of little children; if you mean the evil drink that topples the Christian man and woman from the pinnacle of righteous, gracious living into the bottomless pit of degradation and despair, and shame and helplessness, and hopelessness, then certainly I am against it.
>
> But if when you say whiskey you mean the oil of conversation, the philosophic wine, the ale that puts a song in their hearts and laughter on their lips, and the warm glow of contentment in their eyes; if you mean Christmas cheer; if you mean the stimulating drink that puts the spring into the old gentleman's step on a frosty, crispy morning; if you mean the drink which enables a man to magnify his joy, and his happiness, and to forget, if only for a little while, life's great tragedies, and heartaches, and sorrows; if you mean that drink, the sale of which pours into our treasuries untold millions of dollars, which are used to provide tender care for our little crippled children, our blind, our deaf, our dumb, our pitiful aged and infirm, to build highways and hospitals and schools, then certainly I am for it.
>
> This is my stand. I will not retreat from it. I will not compromise.[1]

That's sort of the way I feel about the cellular phone. If by cellular phone you mean that wonderful device that helps you use time more effectively going from one customer to another, that lets you confirm or change appointments while on the road, that eliminates frustrating searches for a pay phone, that keeps you from having to get out of your car in a dangerous neighborhood at midnight to make an emergency phone call; if you mean the technology that enables you instantly to report a stranded motorist or an accident or a drunk driver, thereby saving precious lives and untold human misery, then certainly I am for it.

But if by cellular phone you mean the umbilical cord that keeps you tied to the office every minute of the day, that makes it impossible to relax while driving because you know there are some things you could be checking on, the gadget that prevents you from delegating effectively because you are now available twenty-four hours a day for consultation on every tiny decision; if you mean the damnable device that takes your mind off your driving while you are arguing with the personnel department, thus increasing the chance that you and others on the road will wind up in a bloody and perhaps fatal accident, then certainly I am against it.

This is my stand. I will not retreat from it. I will not compromise.

Clutter

Many years ago W. C. Fields made a movie in which he was a busy executive, his desk piled high with disorganized papers. One day while he was away from the office, his secretary organized everything into neat stacks. When he returned he needed a particular paper but didn't know which pile it was in, so he stirred everything as if he were tossing a salad, then reached in and triumphantly pulled out the paper he wanted!

That may work in skits, but it doesn't work in the real world. There are some rare executives—Harold Geneen of ITT was one—who can operate efficiently despite an untidy desk, but for most of us clutter drastically diminishes efficiency. (Perhaps a definition is in order here: Clutter doesn't mean a lot of papers on your desk; it means a lot of *unrelated* papers.)

I meet with a lot of resistance on this poinι. Some people argue that all the papers on their desk are "important," that they don't want to risk overlooking any of them by having them out of sight. Nonsense. You can concentrate on only one thing at a time. Select the highest priority item, and put everything else on a side table, with the second most urgent on the top of the pile. Accept the fact that *no matter how important all these projects may be, you can concentrate on only one of them at a time.* The more important the others are, the more distracting they are: Each time they catch your eye you must stop your train of thought, remind yourself that despite their importance you can't do them yet, and then try to regain your momentum on the higher priority task at hand. Some people run this mental obstacle course dozens of times a day!

You should make it a habit to clear your desk completely each evening before leaving the office because it compels you to make some unpleasant decisions. (Remember that a pile of paperwork is usually a pile of postponed decisions.) And it gets the next day off to a better start: Arriving at a cluttered desk is like getting up in the morning to a sink full of dirty dishes. That's no way to begin a day.

And when I recommend clearing your desk *completely* at the end of the day, I mean that literally. Don't just tidy up, putting things in stacks. Something mysterious takes place when you leave two papers on a desk overnight: In the morning there will be four!

Communication

A *frequent cause* of time waste is a lack of clear, direct, germane communication between people.

When Voltaire said, "Words were given to man to enable him to conceal his true feelings," he was describing the world as it too often is rather than as it should be. Too often we communicate with our boss, our fellow workers, or our subordinates in terms of what we think we *should* say or in terms of what we think the other person would like to hear, instead of expressing our real feelings. We pussyfoot and call it tact. We equivocate and call it human relations. We offer mild praise for an unsatisfactory job a subordinate hands us, resolving to put the finishing touches on ourselves instead of explaining that we had expected something different.

A mollycoddling attitude toward subordinates or a pussyfooting demeanor with superiors wastes the time of everyone involved. Open, frank communication is better for everyone concerned, keeping the air clear, avoiding a lot of time-wasting wheel-spinning.

This is not to say that tact doesn't have its place. The basic rule to keep in mind when communicating dissatisfaction is to talk about the *thing* rather than the *person*. Telling an employee he or she is not doing satisfactory work is far less helpful than analyzing specific shortcomings in the project turned in.

The important thing is to make sure that sloppy work by a subordinate does not go unchallenged, because that will increase your own work load and add to your time problems.

A clear statement of what is expected can save a lot of time for everyone concerned. If a subordinate's actions are wasting your time, your best bet is to say so simply and directly. Make it clear to subordinates (and superiors) that you are serious about making the best possible use of your time and need their help.

Commute Time

In large metropolitan areas it is not unusual to spend an hour on the highway or the commuter train getting to work in the morning, and another hour getting home. According to a study by the Federal Highway Administration, the average commute time in the United States is twenty-two minutes each way, and in metropolitan areas with a population of a million or more, 32 percent of commuters live more than thirty-five minutes from work.

Anything that takes that much time out of your life deserves special attention. Obviously, there are two things to consider: (1) Can commute time be reduced and (2) can commute time be used more effectively?

Mr. Jones drives thirty-five minutes to get to work. His friend, Mr. Brown, lives only fifteen minutes from the office. Mr. Jones doesn't think of the difference as being very significant—"only a few more miles, and you get used to it." But do the arithmetic: That twenty-minute difference means forty minutes a day, or three and a third hours per week. Figuring a forty-hour work week, Mr. Jones spends *four weeks more than Mr. Brown every year* in actual driving time!

Commute time should not be the overriding consideration in selecting a home, of course, but it deserves far more consideration than the average family gives it. A difference of "only" five or ten minutes can be a big difference indeed when figured on a cumulative basis. And environmental concerns give everyone an added incentive to take a long, hard look at driving distances.

As for the second point, the most effective use of commute time varies with each person. Listening to whatever happens to be on the car radio is seldom the best way to spend this time. More productive uses might include listening to a cassette designed to increase professional skills; replaying your "Dutch Uncle" tape (the one we mentioned on page xvii); getting your thoughts in order for a morning staff meeting; or analyzing business or personal problems or opportunities. Or it may be that just relaxing to music would be a good use of your time on this particular day. On the other hand, if the weather is bad or the traffic heavy, your best bet, of course, would be to concentrate totally on your driving.

The important thing is to avoid using commute time in a way determined by inertia or by habit. Consciously decide how you would prefer to channel your attention during the trip. You'll be surprised how much can be obtained from those otherwise wasted moments.

Concentration

O*f all the principles* of time management, none is more basic than concentration. In counseling people who are having serious time management problems, I invariably find that they are trying to do too many things simultaneously. When I insist that they must take them up one at a time, they say, "But they are *all* important." And sometimes they are. But they can't be done simultaneously (unless some of them can be delegated, which of course is always worth considering).

The amount of time spent on a project is not what counts: It's the amount of *uninterrupted* time. Few problems can resist an all-out attack; few can be solved piecemeal.

Successful authors learn the importance of concentration. One of the most prolific of modern novelists was the French detective story writer Georges Simenon. Simenon's method was to cut himself off completely from the outside world while working on a book: no phone calls, no visitors, no newspapers, no mail—living, as he said, "like a monk." After about eleven days of total immersion in his writing, he would emerge with another best-selling novel.

Few of us would carry concentration to that extreme, but if we did, who knows what we might accomplish? As Peter Drucker noted in his *Adventures of a Bystander,* "Whenever *anything* is accomplished, it is being done, I have learned, by a monomaniac with a mission."

Oliver Wendell Holmes put it this way: "If you want to hit a bird on the wing, you must have all your will in focus. You must not be thinking about yourself, and, equally, you must not be thinking about your neighbor; you must be living with your eye on that bird. Every achievement is a bird on the wing."

Of course, under some circumstances doing two things at once—"killing two birds with one stone"—makes sense. But some people carry this concept to an extreme in their frantic efforts to get maximum value out of every minute. For example, in one of his famous letters to his son, dated December 11, 1747, Lord Chesterfield said:

> I knew a gentleman who was so good a manager of his time that he would not even lose that small portion of it which the calls of nature obliged him to pass in the necessary house; but gradually went through all the Latin poets in those moments. He bought, for example, a common edition of Horace, of which he tore off gradually a couple of pages, read them first, then sent them down a sacrifice to Cloacina; this was so much time fairly gained.

Well, perhaps. Personally, I believe good time management requires concentrating on one thing at a time, whether in the necessary house or elsewhere.

Conference Calls

The most underused time-saving device, I am convinced, is the conference call.

In case you don't know (and it's surprising how many people don't), the conference call is simply a way of holding a meeting with any number of people, in almost any number of places, via telephone. Of course, it helps if you previously have alerted the people you intend to include so they will be available and will have an idea of what is going to be discussed.

Many who use the conference call to bring together people in several different cities forget that it is equally valuable on a local basis. If you are a PTA president, for example, and have several items you must discuss briefly with your executive committee, you can either call a meeting, which kills the evening for everyone involved, or get everyone together on a conference call and conclude your business within a few minutes at a negligible cost.

An incidental benefit of conference calls: When people know they are going to be charged by the minute, they tend to do their homework ahead of time and are much more concise in their discussion.

Copies

Excessive record-keeping is a symptom of insecurity.

Figure out how often you use the various kinds of material you file. Take each category and ask yourself, "What is the worst thing that could happen if this file didn't exist?" You'll find that most of the time the answer is "Nothing." If you really needed the information, it probably could be located elsewhere in the company in someone else's file. Or a phone call would do the trick, or you would get along fine without it.

This is not to say that comprehensive files aren't useful, but the question is whether they are useful *enough* to justify the amount of time and effort that goes into keeping them current. Estimate the amount of time spent filing such things as old company newsletters, routine memoranda, information copies of other people's memos, and so on, and ask yourself if the company wouldn't be ahead if the same number of hours were put into something directed toward achieving your primary goal.

Correspondence

How *to handle correspondence* quickly and efficiently:

1. Have incoming mail screened and sorted, if possible. If you open your own mail, sort as you open (with waste-basket close at hand).
2. Handle each letter only once. Avoid paper shuffling. Do whatever has to be done (checking, forwarding, phoning, replying) immediately instead of postponing action. A good phrase to keep in mind is the 3-D's: do it, delegate it, or ditch it.
3. If a brief reply is possible, write it on the incoming letter or memo, and fax or mail it back to the sender. Or make a photocopy for the file and return the original.
4. If possible, put your dictation on a tape, belt, or disk (see "Dictating Machines").
5. Use form letters and form paragraphs for routine correspondence.
6. Use electronic mail or voice mail instead of paperwork whenever possible.
7. Don't make frequent revisions. Perfectionism is time-consuming.
8. Get to the point.
9. If you have a long memo, make an outline before dictating.
10. Avoid unnecessary copies. They waste somebody's time to make, distribute, file, or read.
11. For internal correspondence, try "speed-letter" forms with carbons already inserted and with space for a reply.
12. Don't write when a phone call will do. Especially if there is something to be negotiated or ideas to be exchanged, do it by phone or face to face instead of on

paper. Use memos primarily to announce, to remind, to confirm, or to clarify.

13. Use short, terse words. Don't perpetrate polysyllabic obfuscation.

Crises

Whenever you are faced with a crisis, ask yourself, "What can I do to prevent this crisis from recurring?"

Many of the crises that arise in business or in personal life result from failure to act until a matter becomes urgent, with the result that more time is required to do the job. For example, if you are behind schedule with an annual printing job, you can't mail your manuscript to the printer, you must hand-deliver it; you can't wait for proofs to be delivered, you must have someone pick them up; you can't delegate various tasks in connection with the job, you must do them yourself in order to gain time.

Whenever such a crisis occurs, write yourself a note and put it in your "Future" file to appear on the date you should start working.

Failure to start early enough is only one cause of crises. Others include misunderstandings due to unclear communications, lack of periodic status reports that can serve as an early-warning system, failure to follow through after delegating, and failure to make contingency plans.

Analyze each crisis and see if you can devise ways of preventing a repetition. You'll find you can save enough time and energy to enable you to deal effectively with those relatively few cases in which circumstances totally beyond your control make it necessary to push the panic button. It is better to solve problems than crises!

Day's End

Make it a habit to end every workday by doing three things:

1. *Tidy up.* Never sentence yourself to start the next day with the ultimate downer, a messy desk.
2. *Evaluate your day.* Mentally give yourself a grade. Ask yourself such questions as—
   - ☐ Was I proactive or reactive? Did I initiate or just respond?
   - ☐ Did I establish a major goal for the day—and did I reach it? If not, why not?
   - ☐ Did other people intrude unduly on my time, and if so how did I respond?
   - ☐ Was I guilty of wheel-spinning activities at any time during the day?
   - ☐ If I could live this day over, what would I do differently?
3. *Plan the next day's activities.* Don't leave work with only a hazy idea of what you'll do tomorrow. Crystallize your intentions by reducing them to writing. You'll sleep better knowing that you don't have a lot of ill-defined loose ends to take care of, and when you arrive at work tomorrow morning you'll get off to a running start.

Deadlines

You can greatly increase your effectiveness if you simply give yourself a deadline for each task and do your best to stick to it. Most people work better under pressure, and a self-imposed deadline can provide the pressure you need to keep at your task until it is completed. Until you set a deadline for a project, it isn't really an action program; it is more like a vague wish, something you intend to do some day. The problem is that, as someone has pointed out, "someday is not a day of the week."

Remember Parkinson's Law: "Work expands to fill the time available for its completion." It follows that *an assignment to yourself or others should never be open-ended.*

Sometimes it helps to announce your deadline so that other people are expecting you to have the work done by a certain time. This increases your motivation.

If the job is complex, give yourself intermediate deadlines so that you can keep working at a steadier rate instead of having a burst of frantic activity just before the zero hour.

Respect deadlines. If you get into the habit of stretching them, they lose their effectiveness both as a motivator for you and as a spur to the people around you.

Delegation

The *first recorded example* of failure to delegate is found in the eighteenth chapter of Exodus.

Moses, having led his people out of Egypt, was so impressed with his own knowledge and authority that he insisted on ruling personally on every controversy that arose in Israel, a task that kept him busy, as the scriptures say, "from the morning unto the evening." He served as a one-man teacher, general, legislature, small-claims court, district court, and supreme court, to say nothing of his purely ecclesiastical duties. His father-in-law, a wise priest named Jethro, recognized that this was poor use of a leader's time. Speaking as the original management consultant, he said, "The thing that thou doest is not good. Thou wilt surely wear away, both thou, and this people that is with thee: for this thing is too heavy for thee; thou art not able to perform it thyself alone."

We don't know what Moses replied at this point, but I suspect that if some future Dead Sea scrolls are uncovered giving the entire conversation, it will be found that Moses responded

the way most modern executives do, with something like,
"Jethro, thou art absolutely right. I agree with thee one thousand percent. I know that I am wearing myself out, and I
would like to delegate more if I could. But confidentially,
Jethro, thou hast no idea what a bunch of turkeys I have to
work with. Thou simply canst not get competent help these
days!"

In any event, we know that Jethro recommended a two-
phase approach: First, educate the people concerning the laws
and ordinances; second, select capable leaders and give them
full authority over all small or routine matters, thus freeing
Moses to concentrate on major decisions and long-range planning. The advice is still sound. Too many managers, like
Moses, enjoy the feeling of omnipotence that comes from
making all the decisions. Not only is this poor management of
your own time; it also stifles creativity and smothers growth
in subordinates.

You don't have to be a corporation executive to delegate,
either. Parents who don't delegate household chores are doing
a disservice to themselves and their children. Officers of a
volunteer organization owe it to themselves and the organization to spread the blessings of involvement to as many people
as possible. Running a Boy Scout troop can be as time-consuming as running General Motors if you try to do everything
yourself.

One caution: Giving subordinates jobs that neither you nor
anyone else wants to do isn't delegating, it's dumping. And
although it may be necessary at times, it doesn't nourish their
egos, encourage them to grow, or enable them to assume the
decision-making role that can help to free more of your time.
So learn to delegate the challenging and rewarding tasks.

Delegating with strings attached is self-defeating. If you ask
someone to prepare a brochure, for example, don't add a lot
of detailed advice about format, typeface, and illustrations.
People do a better job and take more pride in it if they can
make such choices themselves.

The key to delegation is the word *entrust.* When you delegate, you entrust the entire matter to the other person, along
with sufficient authority to make necessary decisions. This is

quite a different thing from saying, "Just do what I tell you to do," which is treating your subordinates as if they were puppets. Nobody has ever figured out how to motivate a puppet!

DELEGATION: *A PARABLE*

Once upon a time there was a Little Red Hen who owned a wheat field. "Who will help me harvest the wheat?" she asked.

"Not I," said the pig. "I don't know how."

"Not I," said the cow. "I'm too clumsy."

"Not I," said the dog. "I'm busy with some other things."

So the Little Red Hen did it herself.

"Who will help me grind the wheat into flour?" she asked.

"Not I," said the pig. "That is another vocation in which I'm untrained."

"Not I," said the cow. "You could do it much more efficiently."

"Not I," said the dog. "I'd love to, but I'm involved in some matters of greater urgency. Some other time, perhaps."

So she did it herself.

"Who will help me make some bread?" asked the Little Red Hen.

"Not I," said the pig. "Nobody ever taught me how."

"Not I," said the cow. "You're more experienced and could do it in half the time."

"Not I," said the dog. "I've made some other plans for the afternoon. But I'll help you next time."

So she did it herself.

That evening when guests arrived for her big dinner party, the Little Red Hen had nothing to serve them except bread. She had been so busy doing work that could have been done by others that she had forgotten to plan a main course, prepare a dessert, or even get out the silverware. The evening was a disaster, and she lived unhappily ever after.

MORAL: A good leader will find a way to involve others to the extent of their ability. To do the job yourself is the chicken way out.

Deskless Office

The executive desk: a massive mahogany symbol of prestige and power. How could the leader of a corporation get along without one?

Well, very nicely, according to some people who have tried it.

The idea of a deskless office was first promoted many years ago by Lawrence Appley, former chairman of the American Management Association, who contended that "most desks only bury decisions." In recent years the popularity of the concept of "Management by Walking Around," espoused by Tom Peters and others, has caused a renewed interest in the idea of a deskless office. It isn't feasible for most executives, but some have found it works quite well.

One problem with a desk is that it provides a convenient place for papers to pile up, and the executive's attention is soon focused on paperwork instead of on what's happening. By the time a problem has become serious enough to reach the boss in written form, it's often too late to deal with it effectively.

Consider the jobs of a chief executive: to observe, to analyze, to delegate, to encourage, to decide. A desk isn't essential to any of those functions, and in many cases they will be better accomplished in someone else's office or in a meeting or wandering around the plant or sitting in a chair with a clipboard.

Then there's the psychological aspect. When you have a subordinate seated across the desk from you, there is a psychological barrier between you. It's sort of a power play: You are the boss, seated in a position of authority, and the subordinate feels appropriately diminished (if that's what you want—and if you are an insecure leader, it probably is). But a conversational setting without the desk between you creates more of a team atmosphere in which you can exchange ideas and opinions more candidly.

A good analogy is a football coach. The coach doesn't sit in a plush chair, removed from the bench; he sits on the same bench as the players. And he doesn't lose any stature or power by doing so. Instead, he builds rapport and a feeling that although he is the boss, he is part of the team. In today's unpredictable and highly competitive atmosphere, the companies with team spirit are going to be more successful than those where the employees feel like puppets, as they do in a rigidly hierarchical organization.

You may be wondering what all this has to do with time management. Well, the relationships you establish with subordinates will determine to a large extent how you allocate your time, and the more time you spend away from your ivory tower interacting, observing, listening, coaching, and "cheerleading" (to use Tom Peter's phrase), the more effective you will be. You don't have to get rid of your desk to do this, but it can help.

Dictating Machines

I *am appalled*—that's the only word that does it justice—at the number of executives who write out letters and memos in longhand* instead of using a dictating machine.

My informal surveys (taken by a show of hands at time management seminars) indicate that about 60 percent of those who have a secretary to type their letters still use the horse-and-buggy system of a handwritten draft. How archaic! Why should an executive making $80,000 or more a year sit with a yellow pad and a pencil writing ten or fifteen words a minute? One can dictate at five or ten times that speed. In this high-tech world of modems, lasers, laptops, fax machines, scanners, and electronic "mice," the most underutilized time-

---

*This refers only to letters and memos long enough to warrant being typed. The scrawling of a brief informal note often saves time and is to be encouraged—provided the handwriting is legible.

saving device is one that has been around for decades: the
dictating machine.

Why are so many executives so reluctant to dictate? Mike
fright, for one thing: They freeze up when a microphone is in
their hand. Perfectionism, for another: They believe they must
dictate sentences that will be perfect the first time. And disorganized thinking: They don't figure out ahead of time exactly
what points they want to make.

Some tips that will help you overcome dictaphobia:

1. *Make an outline* before you begin dictating. After you
   get the hang of it, you'll generally skip this step, but in
   the beginning it helps immeasurably.
2. *Dictate a draft rather than a final version.* Again, you'll
   eventually discontinue this (at least on routine correspondence), but initially it helps you relax, knowing
   that you can revise as much as you want once you see
   the draft. In other words, don't edit as you dictate. Just
   talk.
3. *Get good equipment,* the best you can afford. Once you
   graduate from the "draft" procedure you can save a lot
   of time by editing on the tape. The newer dictation machines permit you to make changes at the exact spot on
   the tape where an error occurs, without erasing the rest
   of the recording. Also helpful are such things as warn-
   ing signals when you are nearing the end of the tape and
   automatic backup, which repeats the last few words
   each time you resume speaking, giving you a running
   start.

   Consider getting either a microcassette or minicas-
   sette ultracompact portable recorder, which can be carried in a shirt pocket. You'll find yourself using it frequently when away from the office, to make notes while
   driving, and so forth.
4. *Practice.* This is the most important point of all. Your
   reluctance to use this high-payoff, time-saving device
   will disappear as you become more comfortable with it
   through frequent use, and it will become as much a part
   of your daily routine as the telephone.

Efficiency Versus Effectiveness

The day of the old-fashioned "efficiency expert" is long gone. Today, management consultants think in terms of effectiveness, which is a broader and more useful concept.

Efficiency concerns the best ways of doing an assigned job. Effectiveness, on the other hand, concerns the *best use of time*—which may or may not include doing the particular job in question.

For example, suppose you have a list of people you must telephone concerning an upcoming meeting. If you were thinking in terms of efficiency, you would consider when would be the best time to call them, whether their names might be put in your telephone's memory bank in order to save time, whether the list is accurate and current, and so on. But if you were thinking in terms of effectiveness, you would ask yourself if calling these people is what you should be doing right now. You would consider alternative methods of communicating; you would examine the possibility of delegating the task to someone else or perhaps eliminating it altogether so that your time could be used more effectively.

Sound time management involves thinking of effectiveness first and efficiency second. In other words, as someone has noted, doing things right is not as important as doing the right things.

Exercise: The Time Factor

The big health fad of the 1970s and '80s was strenuous exercise, based on Benjamin Franklin's famous observation that "there's no gain without pain." The good news of the 1990s is that it ain't necessarily so. Exercise is important, all right, but we know now that it doesn't have to involve either marathons or masochism.

The jogging craze was started by Dr. Kenneth Cooper, who invented the word "aerobics" and published a popular book by that title in 1968. Soon millions of Americans were donning sweatsuits and pounding the pavement. Many benefited from "going for the burn," but many others just gave up the regimen because it was too demanding, too time-consuming, or too hard on the knees and ankles. Studies showed that only 10 percent of Americans engaged in regular vigorous exercise.

In 1989 the *Journal of the American Medical Association* published results of the most comprehensive fitness study ever conducted, and the findings were good news for those who want to stay healthy and are willing to exercise but don't want to devote a lot of time to it. The study, conducted over fifteen years at Dr. Cooper's Institute for Aerobics Research in Dallas, involving 13,344 men and women, showed that moving out of the "couch potato" category and getting moderate exercise is all that's needed to achieve a dramatic reduction in death rates from heart disease, cancer, and other diseases. Going beyond that and running thirty or forty miles a week provides some additional protection, but not much. You gain dramatic benefits with only thirty minutes of brisk walking or some other aerobic exercise at least every other day.

Important as lowering the death rate is, however, that's not the reason for including this subject in a book on time management. The real reason is that when you plan your day and your week, you should begin by blocking out time for exercise, not just because of the health benefits but because you will then have more "prime time" during the day, more high-output time when you will be "bright-eyed and bushy-tailed." You'll get more done.

Besides, according to a study of seventeen thousand Harvard graduates conducted by Dr. Ralph S. Paffenbarger, Jr., of Stanford University,[1] moderate exercise can add up to two years to a person's life! If that isn't "time management," what is it?

Fear

Procrastination wears many disguises—laziness, indifference, forgetfulness, overwork—but behind the mask, I am convinced, is usually a single emotion: fear. It may be fear of pain (as in postponing a visit to the dentist) or, more commonly, fear of embarrassment, rejection, or failure.

Analyze your fears. Precisely what are you afraid of? Is your fear real or exaggerated? Is there anything you can do to increase your chances of success—getting additional facts, rehearsing a presentation, seeking advice? Fears that have persisted for a long time in the form of vague uneasiness at a subconscious level often dissipate as soon as they are faced squarely and alternatives are honestly examined.

Above all, ask yourself, "What is the worst thing that can happen?" Often it would be only a moment's embarrassment or the need to admit a mistake.

Sometimes, however, the fear will remain. In this case, the key words to remember are *act as if.* Try to picture yourself actually doing the thing you are postponing; "see" yourself making the sales pitch or giving the speech or confronting the hostile committee, and imagine yourself doing it coolly and with self-confidence. Then tell yourself that no matter how much fear you may feel, you are going to act as if you had none. Whether you call this process the self-fulfilling prophecy or psychocybernetics or psyching yourself or merely positive thinking, the fact remains, as millions of people have found, that it works!

Files, Proliferation Of

When Marks & Spencer began its famous war on paperwork (see page 68), it discovered that it was able to abolish two-thirds of its files. After the system had been in effect ten years, a key corporate executive said, "I can only remember two instances when we couldn't find what we wanted." A small price to pay for the elimination of tons of files!

The reason files get out of hand is that we ask ourselves the wrong question when deciding whether or not to file something. We ask, "Is it conceivable that I might want to refer to this again someday?" The answer is always yes (anything is "conceivable"), so we file everything.

Instead of asking that question, use this one: "If I wanted this item again someday and didn't have it, what would I do?" Usually you would get along just fine without it. But if it were really needed, there are usually simple ways of getting it. For example, why maintain a file of the company's employee publications when you know that if you needed a back issue, you could get it by calling the publication office? Why file an announcement from the personnel office that next Monday will be a holiday? Note it on your calendar, then throw away the memo. In the unlikely event that some question arises, you know that a copy is on file in the personnel office, and the worst that could happen would be that you'd have to phone a clerk there for another copy or for the information you need.

Excessive record-keeping is a symptom of insecurity and defensive thinking. It indicates that you are more concerned with documentation than with attaining objectives, more concerned with covering your rear than with making things happen. It's the breeding ground of bureaucracy.

Someone has noted that there is no rearview mirror on a jet plane because the future is coming at you so fast that you have no time to think about where you've been. Life is like that jet plane. Your focus should be on where you're headed and how you're going to get there, rather than on preserving and embellishing the records of where you've been.

Files, Two Thoughts On

1. The general rule is: A few fat files are better than a lot of thin ones.

    It may appear more efficient to have file categories with numerous subdivisions, but the more subdivisions you have, the more chance there is for misfile because of somebody's misinterpretation of the primary subject matter. Sure, it takes a bit longer to go through a fat file to find what you want, but you save more than enough time in filing (and avoidance of errors) to make up for it.

    Within reason, of course.

2. Files, whether electronic or physical, should be the domain of whoever does the filing and retrieving. Bosses should refrain from requiring that specific categories be set up because the minds of bosses and file clerks seldom run in the same channels. (Remember what we said about delegation?)

Flowcharts

A *map* increases your chance of reaching your destination. Similarly, a flowchart increases your chance of reaching your objective.

Like a map, a flowchart shows you what lies between you and your goal, and helps determine the best way to get there.

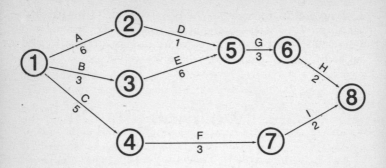

It's useful in planning almost any project and indispensable in planning a really complex one because it depicts in visible form the relationship of various tasks. Although designed primarily to coordinate the work of a number of people, it is equally useful when one person is responsible for performing a complex task and needs a system for setting priorities and monitoring progress.

Most flowcharts are variations of the PERT* system devised by the U. S. Navy for development of the Polaris submarine. A simplified form is shown above. Each circle represents a *milestone* or a *point in time.* For example, in a construction project, circles would represent such events as completion of the floor plan, granting of a permit, completion of the brickwork, and so forth. The lines between the circles, represented by letters, denote *activities* or *processes,* such as the drafting of the floor plan, preparing the paperwork for the permit application, the actual bricklaying, and so on. The number below each line indicates the estimated number of days required for that particular process.

The flowchart thus depicts the relationship among various activities, showing which can be pursued independently and which are contingent upon others—information that is often overlooked in the absence of such a diagram. Furthermore, it makes it possible to determine the "critical path"—the steps

*Performance Evaluation and Review Technique

that will determine how long the overall project will take. For example, in our flowchart the critical path is 1-3-5-6-8. Assuming the time estimates are correct, those steps will take fourteen days, which is how long the entire project will require. If activities A, C, D, F, or I were accomplished in less time, it would have no effect on the final date of completion since the critical path takes fourteen days. If any of those activities took a day or two longer than scheduled, it wouldn't matter, but the gain (or loss) of a day in activities B, E, G, or H would result in a corresponding speedup (or delay) for the entire project.

Obviously, then, the planner initially would give top priority to activity B, which is on the critical path. Without the flowchart the tendency might be to start with A or C in order to get the more time-consuming tasks done first. But to do so would be a serious mistake, creating a bottleneck at milestone 5, thus delaying the entire project.

The flowchart also has another function: It reminds the planner that certain activities, such as A, B, and C (and later, D, E, and F), might possibly be carried on simultaneously—again avoiding the likelihood of a bottleneck occurring because of oversight.

It's true that a picture is worth a thousand words. The flowchart is simply a "picture" of what needs to be done, and it's worth a thousand explanations.

Follow-up

I*f you ask people* to do things and they usually don't get around to them, stop asking yourself, "What's the matter with people these days?" Instead, ask yourself, "What's the matter with *me?* What am I doing (or failing to do) that causes people to give me empty promises?"

Chances are you have been training them to do just that. Whenever you ask someone to do something, whether that person is a subordinate, a co-worker, a friend, or, yes, even your boss, that person generally asks himself or herself what the chances are that the task can be "forgotten"—*based on past experience with you.* If you have established a pattern of invariably following through on assignments, your project is going to get priority treatment. Nobody enjoys having to make excuses. But if there's a pretty good chance, based on past experience, that you won't follow through, your project is likely to wind up on the back burner, maybe permanently.

One way of reminding yourself to follow through, and of gently convincing the other person that you intend to, is to use some kind of form, such as that on the next page, to keep track of assignments and deadlines. Have such a form at hand whenever you attend a meeting; it's an easy way to keep track of what was decided and to avoid misunderstandings about assigned responsibilities. Some supervisors find it useful to post such a list on a unit bulletin board. But in most cases the mere knowledge that such a list exists and that it will be the basis of follow-up action is sufficient to keep things moving.

Remember, though, that following through on requests is only one part of the process. Behavior modification experts emphasize that the most important element in a training situation is what happens when the task is done right, not wrong. So when associates complete an action before the deadline, mention to them that you appreciate their timely response. The behaviorists call this positive reinforcement. Some psychologists call it stroking. Other people call it common courtesy. Whatever you call it, it works wonders.

While some follow-up is essential in any organization, if you find yourself spending too much time checking up on people, something is wrong. In that case, ask yourself these questions:

1. Am I making myself clear? Do I ask for specific actions, or do I phrase requests in ambiguous terms, such as, "I'd appreciate it if sometime you would . . ." or "It might be a good idea to . . ."
2. Do I set a deadline (or better still, get a mutually agreed-upon deadline) whenever I make an assignment?
3. Do I confirm important requests in writing?
4. Do my subordinates understand that I prefer they initi-

Assignment Sheet

Date Assigned	Person Responsible	Action	Due Date	Completed

Relying on an assignment record such as this instead of depending on memory greatly increases chances that tasks you delegate will be performed on time.

ate status reports so that routine follow-through on my part is unnecessary?

5. Do I encourage others to speak up when they question the value of an assignment instead of "forgetting" tasks that they consider unimportant?

Goals

If you want to manage your time better, the first step is to ask yourself this question: "Exactly what are my goals?"

Take a blank sheet of paper. List your personal lifetime goals, the things you would like to be able to look back on by the time you are eighty. Not general things such as to be happy, but specific goals such as a trip to Europe, a master's degree, a savings account balance of a specific figure, a vacation home, a specific weight loss, a working knowledge of Spanish, and so on.

Now list your professional goals, not such generalities as a higher salary or a promotion or greater prestige, but specific things like a salary of a certain amount, promotion to a particular job, or election to a specific office in a professional society.

Then make a list of short-term goals, the things you would like to accomplish in the next six months.

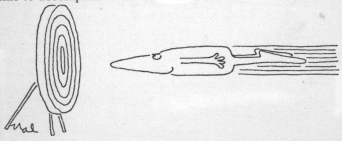

Besides being specific, goals should be attainable and authentic—in other words, *things you really want and are willing to work for.* Keep in mind that they are subject to change at any time; indeed, one of your priority tasks should be to look over your list of goals and update it. But the list should represent your best judgment of what you'd like to accomplish as of this moment.

Now analyze your lists. They probably include more things than you reasonably can expect to do, so assign priorities. Select the three or four goals in each category that you consider most important and write them down someplace where you will see them every day. Memorize them. And a hundred times a day ask yourself, "Is what I am doing now moving me closer to one of my goals?" If the answer is no, figure out some way the activity can be eliminated, delegated to someone else, or downgraded in priority so that it can be accomplished in your least productive time.

One aspect of goal-setting that is often overlooked is setting goals as a couple if you are married or are living with someone. It is seldom done in a systematic, organized way: Every couple has financial discussions, for example, but they usually occur when someone has written a check that bounced. That's not the ideal time for financial planning.

One couple I know has developed a monthly planning session. They set aside the last Friday evening of every month for what they call "a meeting of the Executive Committee." They refuse to accept any social invitations for that evening; they don't turn on the television set. After the kids are in bed, they get out their checkbook and balance it. They go over their financial records and compute their current net worth. They check their lists of goals and discuss how things stand and what changes need to be made, if any, and establish plans and goals for the coming month. They also discuss any conflicts or points of friction that appear to be developing so that they can resolve them in a calm atmosphere. By making a monthly appointment with themselves they avoid the risk of ignoring one of the important aspects of family life.

Indecision: The Paralysis of Analysis

General George Patton summed it up this way: If you have a plan you're 80 percent sure of, "violently execute it."[1]

Timidity is one of the greatest obstacles to achievement, although it always masquerades as something else: prudence, analysis, caution, deliberation. Instead of risking failure (an inherent possibility in any significant decision), it is easier to justify postponing the decision in the name of further fact-finding. Or you tell yourself that it would be better to "sleep on it." But while you're sleeping on it, your competitor is busy, and you wake to find that the opportunity has passed you by.

In their book *CareerTracking*, James Calano and Jeff Salzman call attention to something that most successful people recognize intuitively: *"As strange as it may sound, in professional life it's usually more important to be decisive than it is to be right."*[2] Most errors of judgment can be corrected; lost opportunities for timely action are often lost forever.

·The fact that a choice is difficult should not determine whether it should be made *now;* in fact, the very difficulty of deciding indicates that the matter is of some importance and probably should be resolved as soon as possible. Further study is justified in many cases, of course, but the vast majority of our decisions should be made immediately, making room for action on something else.

It's interesting, incidentally, to look at paperwork in terms of indecision. If you'll go through that stack of paper that has been sitting on your desk for the past few weeks, you'll realize that what you really have is a pile of unmade decisions, many of which could be dealt with in a few seconds if you would just force yourself to make a choice instead of waiting until time or circumstances make the choice for you.

Thomas Watson, Jr., former head of IBM, had this advice

on how to deal with a problem: "Solve it quickly. Solve it right or wrong. If you solve it wrong, it will come back and slap you in the face, and then you can solve it right. Lying dead in the water and doing nothing is comfortable because it is without risk, but it is an absolutely fatal way to manage a business."

Remember, every decision in your life will be made in one of three ways: (1) you will make it yourself, or (2) other people will make it for you, or (3) time will make it for you.

The first way is best.

Information Overload

The copier, the fax, the laptop computer, desktop publishing, electronic mail, online databases, voice mail, modems, computer graphics, cellular phones—all these and many more products of modern technology have one common goal: the production and distribution of more and more information to be absorbed by the human brain. But no one has come up with any ideas for increasing the human brain's capacity to *absorb* more information.

And yet, as sociologist-economist Kenneth Boulding has pointed out, "the crucial element in social systems is not information but knowledge. All a computer does is process information. Knowledge, on the other hand, is obtained much more by the loss of information than by the gain of it. In fact, that's what an organization is all about. Somebody has called an organization a hierarchy of wastebaskets. In other words, a structure to prevent information from reaching the executive desk. Otherwise, the executive gets an information overload."[1]

Sherlock Holmes compared the mind to an attic: "You have to stock it with such furniture as you choose," he told Watson. "A fool takes in all the lumber of every sort that he comes across, so that the knowledge which might be useful to him gets crowded out."

Holmes, for example, professed ignorance of how the solar

system works. He said, "What the deuce is it to me? You say that we go round the sun. If we went round the moon, it would not make a pennyworth of difference to me or to my work."

Holmes was right. Not only is there limited space in your mental attic, but the time available to stock it also is limited. As you scan your morning newspaper, can you really afford to squander precious time on the details of the shooting that occurred yesterday on the other side of town? Or on that profound analysis of why the Lakers outscored the Pistons by two points last night? Or on the revelation that yesterday's stock market fluctuation was caused by a "technical adjustment"? If you consider those bits of information to be precious pieces of furniture you would like to store in your mental attic, by all means do so; but if they are just more intellectual flotsam, why spend time reading about them and then trying to purge them from your mind? Don't let them into the attic in the first place.

Information overload is one of the arguments against speed-reading courses. Even assuming that they do what they claim to do, most people are already taking in more information than they can usefully assimilate. Why multiply the input, especially the input of the kind of material that can be read at several thousand words per minute?

You can cope with the deluge of printed material and junk mail that comes in simply by having your secretary screen out everything that is obviously worthless or by liberal use of the wastebasket as you open your mail. Cancel subscriptions that don't give you enough value for the time you spend reading them. The internal company communications that come across your desk, however, are sometimes more difficult to deal with.

The two most common reasons for excessive internal communication are the following:

1. *Failure to delegate completely.* If subordinates feel that they don't have the authority to handle problems, they invariably pass the buck to their superiors, providing detailed input and then waiting for the decision to be made for them (see "Upward Delegation").

2. *Management by procedures rather than by objectives.*
   When people are judged by how well they comply with
   directives, rather than by how well they meet the organization's objectives, paperwork will multiply—a prolifer-
   ation of memos and reports designed to prove that
   procedures are being followed.

Make it clear to your subordinates that you expect to be
kept informed about progress toward objectives and about
problems requiring your attention. But make it equally clear
that you do not want to be bothered by the submission of
quantities of routine information that will make it difficult for
you to concentrate on the big picture.

Interruptions

You *can't* eliminate interruptions. Most of those interruptions, in fact, are simply requests that you do whatever it is
that you get paid to do. Talking to a customer, answering an
employee's question, responding to a call from your boss—
these are what your job is all about.

Still, you can minimize the number of interruptions, and
you must if you're going to operate effectively because one
hour of concentrated effort is worth more than two hours of
ten- or fifteen-minute segments. It takes time to warm up your
mental motor after an interruption, especially if you return to
the project hours or days later.

So, some suggestions:

1. *Analyze your incoming phone calls, preferably after log-
   ging them for several days.* Are you frequently getting
   calls that have to be referred to other people or that are
   simply unnecessary? Determine what could be done to
   cut down on them.

   For example, a switchboard operator might not know
   what questions to ask of a caller to make sure the call

is referred to the right person. Or perhaps the company's internal telephone directory contains misleading job titles or lists departments in such a way that it is not clear exactly what each department does. Or maybe the directory is not current. These seem to be trifling details, but if they contribute to a pattern of misdirected calls, they should be identified and dealt with.

A more basic cause of unnecessary interruptions, however, is lack of an effective system of communication. If people aren't informed when the new price lists will be published or what the holiday schedule will be or why certain payroll deductions were made, they must interrupt someone, either by phone or in person, to find out.

2. *Use a call-back system for phone calls.* Some people are important enough to be put through any time, but for other calls that don't appear to be emergencies, have your secretary or your answering machine get the name and number so that you can call back at your own convenience. By bunching your calls during a period before lunch or toward the end of the day, when people are less inclined to chat, you can handle calls much more efficiently.

Many people prefer to answer their own phone and to take calls as they come, to demonstrate their accessibility. If this policy fits in with your operating style, fine. But most people will find that the call-back system saves time in the long run.

3. *Set the tone of the conversation at the beginning.* It's possible to answer the phone in a cordial manner, followed by an inquiry such as "What can I do for you?" indicating that while you want to be friendly, you also want to be businesslike. On the other hand, if you simply indulge in pleasantries such as, "It's sure good to hear from you again, how are things going?" you signal that you have time to kill, and the conversation is likely to take many minutes longer. The same principle applies, of course, to personal visits.

4. *Set aside a time for phone calls and consultations.* It can be helpful in an office if people let it be known what times they are available and what times they prefer not to be disturbed. Co-workers understand the need for this kind of arrangement and will not take offense if you explain in advance that you prefer to see people and handle phone calls, for example, before 9:30 and after 11:30, and before 3:00 and after 4:30, thus leaving a substantial block of time in both morning and afternoon to concentrate on major projects. You explain, of course, that this is merely a guideline and that urgent matters should be brought to your attention immediately.

5. If most of your interruptions come from your boss, don't assume that you must put up with them. Pick a judicious time (probably not when an interruption has just occurred!) to explain that you are trying to get better control of your time, and ask if you could arrange mutually convenient times each day to check with each other on routine matters. Chances are your boss will appreciate your interest in operating more effectively and may even get the message that everyone, even the boss, needs to give some thought to time management practices.

Laziness

It's interesting: Nearly everyone will admit to being a procrastinator, but no one wants to be thought of as lazy. And yet the two are often the same thing.

Not always, of course. Procrastination occurs for reasons other than laziness: fear of failure, fear of success, fear of responsibility, guilt, cognitive blocks, environmental factors, and so forth,[1] but one of the most common reasons is just plain laziness, an unwillingness to move out of the comfort zone and tackle the job at hand. It's a fault that is guaranteed to produce failure because no amount of brilliance can overcome inactivity. Bill Bernbach put it this way: "In this world, good doesn't drive out evil. Evil doesn't drive out good. But the energetic displaces the passive."[2]

The trouble is, overcoming laziness seems to involve a Catch-22: The laziness itself hinders you from taking the steps necessary to overcome it. But don't lose hope. Laziness can be conquered.

The first step is to stop viewing yourself as a victim of some uncontrollable deficiency. You must stop thinking, "I just can't make myself get to work on this task." The self-fulfilling prophecy is as immutable as the law of gravity, and you are using it against yourself, reinforcing a habit you want to eradicate. Instead, tell yourself, "I *can* make myself do this task, and I will." Visualize yourself actually doing it. Make it a detailed mental rehearsal, seeing yourself actually performing every phase of the activity, remembering the psychological law that "images or mental pictures and ideas tend to produce the physical conditions and the external acts that correspond to them."

Next, visualize yourself enjoying the fruits of your labor. Give yourself a mental pat on the back for (mentally) doing the task. Decide on some token reward that you will give yourself when the task (or one phase of it) is completed. You'll deserve it because you will have scored a victory, and in the words of Plato, "The first and greatest victory is victory over self."

Next, wash your face with cold water, take three deep breaths, and . . . start. And having started, maintain your momentum.

Nothing is more essential to success than self-discipline, and the good news is that you can achieve it by changing the mental picture you have about yourself and acting accordingly.

Leverage

L*everage* is what makes it possible for a one-hundred-pound person to jack up a ten-ton truck. It can also make it possible for a small investment of time to produce a tremendous pay-off.

To leverage your time you must recognize that when you have a list of things to do, they aren't all of equal importance or even of approximately equal importance. Some are *infinitely* more important than others. We all accept that fact at an intellectual level, of course, but in practice we don't. It's much more fun to cross off six items on a list (even though they're minor) than one item (even though it's far more important in the long run). So we go for the numbers.

This tendency illustrates the Pareto Principle, named after Vilfredo Pareto, an Italian economist-sociologist of the late nineteenth century, who noted that in almost any group of things or people there is a vast difference between the "critical few" and the "trivial many."

It is also known as the 80/20 rule. Thus, in a sales force 20 percent of the salespeople will bring in about 80 percent of the new business; in a discussion group 20 percent of the participants will make about 80 percent of the comments; in a company 20 percent of the employees will account for about 80 percent of the absenteeism; and in a classroom 20 percent of the students will require about 80 percent of the teacher's efforts.

This certainly applies to time. About 80 percent of the pay-off from your daily "To Do" list will relate to just 20 percent of the things listed—often just a single item. To leverage your time you must focus on that task, even though it may lack urgency, as it so often does. So when faced with a choice, instead of opting for the easiest task or the most urgent or the most insistent or the most satisfying, ask yourself, "Which of these tasks will affect my career? Which will alter the bottom

line? Which will matter the most five years from now? Which
relates most directly to my goals?"

And remember that leverage works in both directions: An
enormous investment of time and effort on a low-payoff task
will produce negligible results—which is why doing the right
things is even more important than doing things right.

Lists

I *recommend* keeping two lists for each day—preferably on
the same sheet of paper.

On one side of the sheet (or in your appointment book) list
those items scheduled for a specific time, such as meetings
and appointments. On the other side put your "To Do" list, a
random listing of everything you would like to accomplish
during the day. Then look over your "To Do" list and identify
the one thing that will have the greatest payoff in the long run
(*not* the thing that is most urgent!). Schedule a block of time
(preferably prime time) to work on that high-payoff task.
Then plan to do the others in order of priority as time permits.
Don't schedule secondary tasks for specific times; you need
to maintain enough flexibility to handle unexpected interruptions. Otherwise, your plan will be impractical and you will
become discouraged.

One serious limitation of a "To Do" list is that it is usually
compiled on the basis of urgency. It includes things that de-
mand immediate attention, some of which are important and

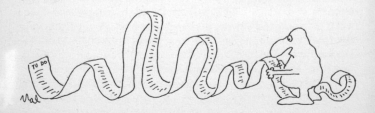

some of which are not; but *it usually does not include the things that are important but not urgent,* such as long-range planning and major projects that you want to accomplish but that nobody is pushing you to do.

So always, when making up your daily list of things that need to be done, take a moment to review your list of objectives (see "Goals") and see if the things you are working on are really the things that will get you closer to where you want to be.

Chances are you won't get to the bottom of your "To Do" list by the end of the day, but don't let that worry you. If you've worked according to priorities, you've accomplished the important things, and that's what time management is all about.

One word of caution, however: When you find yourself transferring an item from today's list to tomorrow's list more than once or twice, it may be that it is a low-priority item, but it also may be that you are procrastinating. In that case, instead of holding it over again, admit to yourself that you're goofing off and figure out what to do about it (see "Procrastination").

Lunch Hour

The *"business" lunch is* a time trap. It is based on the theory that if you break bread with someone, you have the inside track to that person's pocketbook, ideas, or affection, whichever it is you're after.

The theory has some validity, and meeting someone for lunch can be a way of using time effectively. Too often, however, it is counterproductive. It tends to run to two hours, including travel time. It usually involves eating more heavily than usual (including perhaps a martini or two), contributing to midafternoon torpor. And it usually involves doing in two hours what could be accomplished in twenty minutes.

A far better use of time usually is a light lunch and a brisk walk. Even a brief nap, if you can be so lucky.

A practice that many people find useful is to postpone lunch until 1 P.M. or later, using the noon hour for work. In most offices, phone calls and other interruptions are less likely then—and you have the added bonus of quicker service at the cafeteria or in a restaurant when the rush hour is over.

MBO: A Reappraisal

"**M**anagement by objectives," says Tom Peters, "is one more great idea that has been neutered by bureaucrats in nine out of ten applications."[1]

Consultant Peter Drucker coined the term Management by Objectives in 1954. In the decades since, it has become the basic management tool in countless well-run institutions, many of which call it by other names. It works. But in some organizations progress has been slow, as Peters indicates, because MBO threatens the three basic underpinnings of a bureaucracy: tradition, centralized control, and red tape.

MBO means thinking in terms of specific goals rather than in terms of procedures and regulations. It encourages the asking of such questions as "Exactly what are we trying to accomplish?" and "Why should we be doing this?" and "Is there a better way?" instead of such questions as "Is this in keeping with agency policy?" or "Is this what we were told to do?" or "Will this enable our division to hire more people and have more power?"

Setting specific goals and allocating time to those activities that contribute most toward their realization are the keys to effectiveness in any organization, large or small. To use Laurence J. Peter's explanation: "Lacking an adequate objective, a typical management response is to increase input—hire more people, upgrade qualifications, urge employees to work harder. Lacking an objective that defines what the process must do, individuals may increase input and become busily engaged in useless motions producing enormous activity to accomplish nothing."[2]

Individuals as well as organizations easily become preoccupied with process. The sales rep who faithfully makes calls on old customers long after their accounts have ceased to be productive; the teacher who grades a paper on its neatness instead of its content; the supervisor who judges subordinates by how few waves they make rather than by how many ideas they have; and the administrator who requires voluminous written reports on a project instead of checking personally to find out how it's going are some of the people who squander their own time and that of others because they have lost sight of ultimate objectives. Instead, they are thinking in terms of keeping people busy, maintaining a system, and putting up a good front.

To implement MBO in your organization:

1. Prepare a concise mission statement clarifying the organization's overall objectives. Make sure that key people understand where they and their activities fit into the "big picture."
2. Establish a hierarchy of objectives in which each level's objectives support those of the level above it. But—and this is important—negotiate those objectives in a give-and-take session with the people involved instead of laying them down as an ultimatum.
3. Conduct periodic reviews to make sure objectives are being met. The atmosphere should be such that people feel they are being coached, not judged.
4. Don't let the process stifle risk-taking and innovation. MBO must be flexible enough to adapt to changing circumstances.

Meetings: Before

The most important part of a meeting is what happens before it even starts, the preliminary planning that too often is done haphazardly or not at all.

Before the meeting you should take the following steps:

1. ASK YOURSELF IF A MEETING IS REALLY NEEDED.

Remember that people can't meet and work at the same time. Are you meeting as a substitute for action? Are you meeting out of habit instead of need? Could you get together with someone informally in the hallway and accomplish your purpose? Could you meet by conference call? Would electronic mail or fax or a written memo be a more efficient way of distributing the information?

If your meeting is primarily for one-way communication such as an announcement or a status report or motivational presentation to a large number of people, don't overlook the option of videotape. The advantages are obvious: You can make the video at your convenience, and viewers can watch it at their convenience; it can be edited if necessary; and it's a permanent record that can be replayed as often as needed. Or you may want to combine the video with a live conference: Many organizations now begin their weekly staff meetings with videotaped remarks from the CEO or another top executive, often in a different city.

2. KEEP SIZE TO A MINIMUM.*

Someone has noted that the probability of getting off the subject varies with the cube of the number present. In other words, there is a very big difference between a meeting of five people and a meeting of six. That sixth person—the one you are unsure whether or not to invite—is the one who is most likely to get you off the track because he is not as directly involved as the others (that's why you're debating whether to invite him), and since he hates to have his time wasted, he is the one most likely to introduce extraneous subjects into the discussion.

*This assumes that the session is for problem-solving with a give-and-take atmosphere, as distinguished from a meeting intended merely to impart information, in which case it can be as large as needed.

In a problem-solving meeting the optimum size is from four to seven. When you get a group as large as ten or twelve, effectiveness goes out the window: You have separate conferences taking place at opposite ends of the table, or you have one or two dominant personalities taking over and making speeches while the less assertive (but possibly more astute) participants clam up.

If it isn't necessary to have everyone there for the entire meeting, structure it so that some participants come for only a portion or leave early. And when you are asked to attend a meeting, get advance permission to leave as soon as matters you are involved in have been covered.

3. *PROVIDE AN AGENDA IN ADVANCE.*

Your agenda should indicate what you hope to decide, not just what you want to discuss. For example, if you invite several people to your office to "discuss" product lines, you are, in effect, asking them to come and chat. Consider, instead, the effect of an invitation like this:

To: F. Jones, R. Brown, J. Roberts, M. Johnson
Subject: Product lines

I would like to have you or your representative attend a one-hour meeting in my office on Tuesday at 3 P.M. to decide the following regarding product lines:

1. Is our product mix becoming too complex for efficient marketing?
2. Would significant economies result from decreasing the number of package sizes?
3. Would the market accept this?
4. If we cut product lines or sizes, which ones should be first?

Those receiving such a message will come to the meeting knowing exactly what information is expected, and they are likely to have done some thinking and some homework.

One more tip: Consider the format of the above agenda. By putting the agenda in question form you increase interest and provoke thought. That same agenda in traditional format would read:

> Product mix
> Packaging
> Market acceptance
> Priorities

It would be hard to envision a duller agenda than that, whereas the same agenda in question form encourages responses. So remember, for a meeting at which decisions are to be made, always put your agenda in question form. Questions elicit response. Topics do not.

4. CONSIDER SCHEDULING A STAND-UP MEETING OR A WALKING MEETING.

Many companies have now set aside at least one conference room for stand-up meetings. There are no chairs in the room, only a conference table, usually raised to elbow height. Such rooms are popular because people who sit most of the day welcome a chance to do some of their work standing. Stand-up meetings are livelier and shorter than sit-down meetings.

Another option is to combine a meeting and a brisk walk, which some executives believe stimulates creativity. This isn't a new idea: According to a writer in the *Wall Street Journal,* "Protagoras, who conducted a school of practical knowledge in the fifth century B.C. in Greece, gave seminars while walking with his students. Jesus' admonition that those who walked with him would see the light plainly describes a preferred communications method and its benefits. Albert Einstein liked to walk with colleagues when exploring thorny issues of science and morality, and Harry Truman took a daily conversational walk with whichever of his guests or advisers could keep up with him."[1]

Some executives now go even further and hold meetings

while running. They say it helps people relax, gives a better perspective, and helps to "develop a bond that you are not going to develop sitting across the desk."[2]

Meetings on the move. It may be an idea whose time has come!

Meetings: During

Now that you've taken all the steps suggested in the preceding chapter, the meeting itself is a piece of cake. Just remember three things:

1. *START ON TIME.*

Starting on time sets the tone for a brisk, businesslike meeting. Starting late sets the tone for a meeting that will ramble from one subject to another with little being accomplished. A meeting that starts ten minutes late will usually end an hour late.

I've seen many techniques used for dealing with the perennial latecomer. In some organizations the last one to arrive is responsible for taking and distributing notes of the meeting. Sometimes he or she is required to get coffee for the group or is fined. Sometimes the most important and most interesting items are put first on the agenda to penalize latecomers. Secretaries are sometimes given the responsibility of getting their bosses to the meeting on time.

Any of these ideas may work, but there is a simpler way. You don't need to plead, threaten, reprimand, bribe, cajole, or punish—*just start on time!*

The reason people come late to meetings is usually that they have learned from experience that the meeting is going to start late. Let them learn from experience that it will start on time and that if they are not there, they will have to find out what they missed.

2. STAY ON TRACK.

You've taken the trouble to prepare an agenda. Use it. Even if you aren't in charge of the meeting, you can use the agenda to stifle the person (and there's one in every meeting) who wants to get onto extraneous subjects. Speak up!

3. SUMMARIZE.

Before a meeting is adjourned, the person who called the meeting should summarize briefly what has been decided and what assignments have been made. If he or she fails to do so, do it yourself. You'll be surprised how many people will reach for a pencil and make notes of things they have already forgotten.

Meetings: After

Aside from the obvious follow-up there's just one thing to do after the meeting is over, but it's important and is often overlooked: *Distribute minutes promptly.*

Perhaps "minutes" isn't quite the right word. We're not talking about formal minutes, which aren't necessary in the ordinary problem-solving meeting, but rather a memo of confirmation, listing as briefly as possible what was decided.

To demonstrate the need for a written summary, two British psychologists, J. Blackburn and E. J. Lindgren, tape-recorded a discussion at the end of a meeting of the Cambridge Psychological Society. Two weeks later they asked the attendees to write down whatever they could recall about the discussion. The results:

☐   The average number of points remembered by each person was only 8.4 percent of those actually recorded.

☐ Forty-two percent of the items remembered were incorrectly remembered—and substantially so.
☐ Many of the things "remembered" were not said at all or were said on some other occasion![1]

If you want the decisions of your meeting to be carried out, you must take the trouble to write and distribute a record. But the briefer the better—maybe just a sentence or two confirming the following:

1. what was decided
2. what assignments were made
3. the deadlines for action.

Meetings: Stimulating Input

I*f time* spent in staff meetings seems to be unproductive, here's a way of blasting out of the rut you're in: *Require each person to bring two ideas for making his or her own work or the department's work more productive—or ideas that will help the organization as a whole.* You'll be astounded by the results. Not only will a lot of valuable ideas surface, but the atmosphere of the meetings—and of the entire organization—will change.

In 1989, Martin Edelston, president of Boardroom, Inc., began using this technique in his company at the suggestion of Peter Drucker. He starts every staff meeting by asking the attendees for their suggestions. "We all know that we are allowed to 'pass' when our turn comes if we have no ideas to offer," he says, "but no one does—and the flow of ideas has increased rather than decreased as the program has gained momentum."[1]

To instill a fun atmosphere, Edelston strikes a big gong or honks a hunter's horn for each suggestion offered. He also has a stack of dollar bills handy and awards at least $1 for every idea, good or bad. That token amount helps to create a freewheeling, informal attitude. "Our seventy team members now generate about seventy new ideas a week to improve performance," he says. "About half of the ideas are good enough to be acted upon, and some are really great. Some are embarrassing because they are so good, and so obvious that it's hard to see why we hadn't done something about them before." Edelston says that acting immediately on the suggestions, many of which affect the day-to-day work environment, demonstrates to team members that top management cares, and team spirit soars. In addition, each person's mind-set changes from being a defender of the status quo to being an advocate of constructive change.

Meetings are thus made more productive and more fun. That's good time management. It's also good business.

Meetings: The When

I'm often asked my opinion on when is the best time for the weekly staff meeting. My answer is simple: Ask the people involved. They know better than anyone else when would be the most convenient time for them, and not to consult them on something so basic is, in my opinion, rather high-handed.

Having said that, I think it might be well to note that Monday mornings are usually not the best time to hold a weekly meeting.

Some executives like to schedule a staff meeting first thing Monday morning to plan what should be accomplished during the week, but as consultant Jeffrey Mayer points out, "If you wait until Monday to make those decisions, it's already too late. The race has started; everyone else is off and running, and you're still planning. Monday morning staff and sales meetings can take the life, heart, and enthusiasm out of the organization. If the meeting ends after 11:00 A.M., the entire morning may be wasted. Everybody will kill time until they go to lunch. This isn't a very productive way to start a week."[1]

Friday afternoons, of course, are also bad. With the weekend about to begin, people's minds (and sometimes their bodies) are elsewhere.

My personal preference for a weekly meeting is Tuesday, Wednesday, or Thursday afternoon. Mornings are peak performance times for most people, and it's usually best to spend peak time doing, not deliberating.

But taking all this into consideration, seek input from those involved. People appreciate the opportunity to have their say even if they don't get their way.

Meetings: Formal

In the preceding chapters we've been talking mainly about the informal problem-solving meeting, the kind that is most common in business organizations. But meetings of associations, stockholders, boards of directors, commissions, councils, clubs, chambers of commerce, churches, social organizations, conventions, and volunteer groups of various kinds are another matter entirely. To get things done in meetings where motions must be made and voted upon, and where things like amendments and "moving the previous question" keep popping up, it's necessary to know a little about parliamentary procedure.*

A few tips that can help you get things done more quickly and efficiently in formal meetings:

☐ Don't waste time taking unnecessary votes. Whenever anything noncontroversial is proposed, use general consent ("If there is no objection, we will . . ." and so forth). But be sure to use that phrase, providing an opportunity

---

*Sometimes referred to (incorrectly) as "Robert's Rules." *Robert's Rules of Order*, originally intended as a vest-pocket summary of parliamentary procedure, has now grown to a mammoth tome of more than six hundred pages. The most readable explanation of the rules of meetings is *The Standard Code of Parliamentary Procedure*, Third Edition, by Alice Sturgis (McGraw-Hill, 1988).

for objection. If anyone objects, you do not have general (that is, unanimous) consent, and a vote must be taken.

☐ Don't waste time unnecessarily seconding motions. In a general meeting a motion requires a second, but in a committee or board meeting a second is not required.

☐ Don't be unduly formal in committee or board meetings. In an assembly the presiding officer is supposed to be neutral and does not make motions or express opinions on controversial issues, but in a committee or board meeting this does not apply. The person chairing a committee or board can make a motion or participate in debate the same as anyone else—and should, to facilitate decision-making.

☐ Don't try to work out details of a proposal in a large meeting. It can't be done efficiently. Instead, move that the matter be referred to a committee.

☐ When presiding, don't try to speed things up by arbitrarily limiting discussion on a controversial issue. Only the membership can limit or close debate—and only with a two-thirds vote.

☐ Keep minutes brief. Some organizations must keep very detailed minutes for legal reasons, but most minutes are far more detailed than needed, which makes them boring and time-consuming. In general, they should be a record of what was *done*, not what was said.

☐ If you are going to preside over a formal meeting, take time beforehand to refresh your understanding of the procedures by listening to some tapes or by doing some reading. In the words of the noted parliamentarian George Demeter, "It is the duty of the presiding officer to know the rules of parliamentary law and basic parliamentary practice. There is nothing more pitiable than one who is ignorant of parliamentary law trying to preside over an assembly; the more intelligent the assembly, the sadder the spectacle."[1]

Memoranda

When the mail is disposed of we have what is known as Memorandum Hour. During this period everyone sends memoranda to everyone else. If you happen to have nothing in particular about which to dictate a memorandum, you dictate a memorandum to someone, saying that you have nothing to suggest or report. This gives a stimulating exchange of ideas, and also helps to use up the blue memorandum blanks which have been printed at some expense for just that purpose.

—ROBERT BENCHLEY,
From Nine to Five

Memo-writing, whether done by typewriter, pencil, dictation, word processor, or electronic mail, can be a vicious time-waster. Aside from the time it takes to dictate, type, edit, retype, transmit, read, answer, and file, there is another peril: It often encourages procrastination. By writing a memo saying that you are in the process of performing a certain task, you trick yourself into believing that things are moving, that you have done something. There is then less pressure to get on with the job, now that you've gained some breathing time. But pressure is what you need, right?

Another thing to remember is that written communication tends to be one-way. Unless the other person responds in writing, you don't get the feedback you need—the reactions, questions, suggestions, and arguments that ensure your ideas are understood and are sound.

Remember, too, that people are less candid in writing than in discussion. There is a permanence about the written word that encourages caution and restraint. If you want a frank appraisal of someone's work, for example, you would be foolish to ask for a memo or even to rely too heavily on a written

personnel report. A more honest evaluation will always be obtained through a phone call.

And think of the time you save!

So avoid using the memo to carry on dialogue, to negotiate, to determine consensus. It generally should be used only to announce, to confirm, to clarify, to remind.

Mental Blocks

When you keep trying to get a job done and nothing happens, stop. Instead of investing more time in a futile effort, analyze the problem and see if you can come up with a new approach. Usually your frustration will be caused by one of the following:

1. *Lack of facts.* If you aren't sure you have all the facts, you naturally hesitate to write that report, prepare that speech, or plan that campaign. Do some more research and see if it doesn't get you off dead center.

2. *Lack of conviction.* Maybe you are finding it impossible to get started because deep down you don't believe in the value of the task or the way in which you've been told to do it. Instead of letting this uneasiness gnaw away at you, face the facts squarely, analyze the pros and cons,

and confront your boss with a recommendation for a different course of action. If you lose and it's a minor matter, get it done as quickly as possible so you can forget it. If it's a major matter and part of a recurring pattern, better try to find another boss.

3. *Lack of a starting point.* Maybe the task is so overwhelming that you can't figure out how to get started. Use the "salami technique" (see "Procrastination").

4. *Tunnel vision.* Perhaps you are so close to the problem that you can't get a good perspective on it. Get some input from other people. Whether they have any good ideas or not, merely explaining the situation to them often will clarify your own thinking and may stimulate you to find the way out yourself.

5. *Fatigue.* Creative thinking cannot be forced. If you are working on a problem and are getting nowhere, your best bet often is to put it on the back burner overnight and let your subconscious mind take over. Sometimes the answer will come when you least expect it—even in the middle of the night. (The late Henry Kaiser made it a practice to "assign" his subconscious mind a problem to work on just before going to sleep. He found that the answer often came to him at around 3 A.M. He always kept a pencil and piece of paper on the nightstand to scribble a word or two so that he could go back to sleep without worrying about forgetting.)

   But before you postpone action because of fatigue, remind yourself that the symptoms of fatigue and laziness are hard to distinguish. Make sure your inaction isn't due to the most insidious mental block of all, which is—

6. *Lassitude.* Recognize that your doing something shouldn't be determined by whether you *feel* like doing it.

   Le Baron Russell Briggs, a distinguished dean at Harvard University, once asked a student why he had failed to complete an assignment.

   "I wasn't feeling very well," the student explained.

   "Mr. Smith," said the dean, "I think that in time you

may perhaps find that most of the work of the world is done by people who aren't feeling very well."

Those are words worth remembering the next time you put off doing something simply because you are "indisposed."

Naps

There is nothing sacred about the pattern of sleeping eight hours and remaining awake for all of the remaining sixteen. The twenty-four-hour day is simply an accident of astronomy, and most animals have sense enough to take a nap whenever they feel like it, day or night.

Einstein made a nap part of his daily routine. So have countless other well-known figures, including Napoleon, Edison, Churchill, Truman, John D. Rockefeller, General George Marshall, Buckminster Fuller, Eleanor Roosevelt, and Margaret Thatcher.

Many business executives similarly find that a daily nap dramatically increases their energy level. After a heavy lunch the late Malcolm Forbes would often "schedule a conference"—his euphemism for a nap on his office couch. Armand Hammer claimed to have developed the ability to take a ten-minute nap "anywhere at all" by shutting his eyes and imagining himself lying in a forest, listening to a babbling brook. Billionaire John D. MacArthur, who slept only a few hours each night, took a nap whenever he felt like it during the day and felt that it greatly increased his effectiveness.

The benefits of a nap aren't limited just to greater productivity, either. There are measurable health benefits. A recent Greek study of patients with acute heart attacks suggests that a daily thirty-minute nap may reduce the chance of recurrence by almost a third.

When people feel drowsy during the afternoon, they usually attribute it to a heavy lunch or to a sleepless night, but research indicates that there is a strong biological readiness to drowse in midafternoon even among those who have skipped lunch or who have had a full night's sleep. "It seems nature definitely intended that adults should nap in the middle of the day, perhaps to get out of the midday sun," says William Dement, director of the Sleep Disorders Clinic and Research Center at Stanford University.

Finding a suitable physical setting for a nap is, of course, a problem for most people. You need quiet and seclusion, and to get the maximum benefit you should be able to take off your shoes and lie down. (Dozing at your desk doesn't do much for either your nervous system or your reputation!) When you remove your shoes and lie down, you signal to your body that it's time to disengage mentally and physically from your work and just recharge the batteries.

If you can't seclude yourself at the office or go home for a nap, a YMCA or private club may be the answer. Even driving to a nearby park and taking a short nap in the car provides a worthwhile break for some people.

A siesta isn't for everyone, but if you're one of those who perk up after one, arrange your schedule accordingly. You may find you agree with Ogden Nash, who wrote, "I would not trade my daily swoon for all the rubies in Rangoon."

No

O*f all the time-saving* techniques ever developed, perhaps the most effective is the frequent use of the word *no*.

You cannot protect your priorities unless you learn to decline, tactfully but firmly, every request that does not contribute to the achievement of your goals.

The tendency of many time-pressured people is to accept grudgingly new assignments in volunteer organizations, new social obligations, new chores at the office, without realistically weighing the cost in time. Such people worry about offending others—and wind up living their lives according to other people's priorities.

At work, of course, you cannot always turn down the request that you take on a job you think is a waste of time. But you can win a good percentage of the time if you try. Point out to your boss how the new task will conflict with higher-priority ones and suggest alternatives. If your boss realizes that your motivation is not to get out of work but to protect your time to do a better job on the really important things, you'll have a good chance of avoiding unproductive tasks. But you have to speak up. Remember, every time you say no to something, you make it possible to say yes to something else.

Overstaffing

"**M**any hands make light work," my mother used to say when she wanted help with the dishes. But in an office it ain't necessarily so. Many hands make work, period.

Suppose you are a conscientious worker in an office where there isn't enough important work to keep everybody busy. What do you do? Because you want to feel useful, you begin looking for tasks that might have at least some marginal value. You could arrange a survey, prepare a questionnaire, update the policy manual, reorganize the filing system, change the standard personnel forms, generate some red tape, set up a committee, call a meeting, anything to hide from yourself and others the fact that you are not busy on something important.

Or if you can't find something constructive to do, you might simply undertake a vendetta against some other department or person. After all, if you're in a nonessential slot, you are vulnerable, and you'd better get your licks in first.

All of this turbulence and make-work is a result of having too many people in the organization. In a lean organization, people are too busy for trivia, so they don't have these problems.

Well, not to the same extent, anyway.

Paperwork, Cost Of

People who can't understand the importance of simplifying procedures in order to save time can sometimes see the picture better when it is put in terms of saving money.

Suppose that you are running a small business and must hire one additional clerk, at a salary of $300 per week, to cope with unnecessary record-keeping, filing, correspondence, and other paperwork. Suppose that you operate at a profit of 5 percent of sales. That means that you must sell an additional $312,000 worth of merchandise just to pay the salary of that clerk—and that doesn't include fringe benefits.

To put it another way, remember that every reduction in cost is a 100 percent addition to net profit. And elimination of time-consuming reports, filing procedures, excessive written communications, and other unnecessary paperwork is a good place to start. Too often cost-cutting efforts are limited to such obvious targets as new equipment, advertising budget, travel, and turning out the lights, and too little attention is paid to ways of saving money by saving time.

"Time is money," according to the old maxim. You'd better believe it.

Paperwork: The Marks & Spencer Experience

A *number of years* ago Sir Simon Marks, who was then chairman of Marks & Spencer, Britain's most prosperous retail chain, noticed the lights burning in one of his retail stores long after closing. He discovered that two employees were working overtime on stock cards. He investigated and learned that nearly a million such cards were filled out each year and sent to London to keep track of inventory. He ordered a study to determine whether the cards were really necessary. It turned out that they were not; a simpler way of keeping inventory was developed, involving spot checks and (horror of horrors!) even going as far as letting the stockroom clerk look at the shelves and simply reorder when supplies of certain items were getting low.

The success of this effort caused the company to launch the most massive war on paperwork Britain had ever seen. Every form used by the company, every file, every paperwork-creating procedure was scrutinized, and the staff was told to ask, "Would our entire business collapse if we dispensed with this?" The motto was "If in doubt, throw it out."

Within a year, 26 million cards and sheets of paper, weighing 120 tons, had been eliminated. Time cards, for example, were abolished, a million of them a year. Supervisors were trusted to know who was putting in a good day's work and who wasn't.

The Marks & Spencer campaign was no flash in the pan. Effective use of time through simplification and elimination of paperwork has been the guiding principle of the firm ever since, and it has worked.[1]

Essential to the Marks & Spencer type of operation is a realization that people can be trusted, that managers will manage better if given freedom within general guidelines instead of being required through reports and manuals to comply with detailed instructions. Another cornerstone of the philosophy is the idea of "sensible approximation," which means that getting figures close enough for all practical purposes is more efficient than striving after perfection for its own sake.

Companies in the United States and elsewhere have studied and profited by the Marks & Spencer experience. CBS, for example, undertook a thorough housecleaning of its record-keeping system a few years ago and was able to eliminate 15 million pieces of filed paper. One major oil company managed to eliminate two-fifths of its records and cut expenditures for new file cabinets from $20,000 to $5,000 a year.

Examine the paperwork in your own office and see if every report, every multiple copy, every questionnaire, every file, really justifies the time and energy it requires. Then apply Sir Simon's rule: If in doubt, throw it out!

Paperwork Quiz

The old saying, "A place for everything, and everything in its place," applies particularly to paperwork because having a well-established routine makes it possible to concentrate on the content of the message instead of worrying about how you will keep track of it.

The purpose of this quiz is not to help you come up with a right answer because there are no *right* answers. One person might give a certain paper to a secretary, another might put it in a desk file, and both are "right" if they act out of habit, having set up a system instead of having to agonize over the decision. So answer these questions quickly, indicating not what you *should* do but what you probably *would* do. If you have to think about it for a while or if you probably would set the item aside and come back to it later, put a question mark. More than two or three question marks suggests that you need to set up a better system for handling paper work.

Where would you put this paper?

1. Bill for materials you have purchased.

2. Trade journal. Appears to have articles worth reading, but you don't have time to read them now.

3. Memo from your boss asking you to attend a meeting next Monday.

4. Questionnaire from a business school asking your opinion on personnel practices.

5. Material from a subordinate that you will use in preparing your next monthly report of activities.

6. Letter requiring a prompt answer, but you are going to have to make some phone calls before you can answer it.

7. Form letter from a person you call frequently, giving new address and phone number.

8. Memo from another division of your organization, asking for copies of a report prepared by your department.

9. Brochure from a company sell-
ing business forms. You think some
of the forms may be worth ordering,
but you are not sure. _____

10. Letter of complaint from a customer. _____

11. Memo from personnel department concerning procedure for personnel evaluation. _____

12. Note you have written to yourself as a reminder to start sooner
next year on budget preparation. _____

Although there are no *right* answers to the questions in the
foregoing quiz, some discussion is in order because there are
some *wrong* answers that clearly violate principles of effective
time use:

1. If you don't have a firm routine for handling bills, you
   really have problems (and so do your creditors). The
   main thing is to get the bill off your desk by paying it
   or by bucking it to someone else for prompt payment
   or by getting it into a "Future" file for payment at a
   later date.
2. Whatever you do, don't leave the magazine sitting on
   your desk where it will tempt you away from higher-
   priority tasks. Have a separate place, on a side table or
   in a drawer, for reading material.
3. If this memo lists only the time and date of the meeting, the information should be noted on your desk calendar (or pocket calendar), and the memo should be
   thrown away. Otherwise it clutters up files and wastes
   filing time. On the other hand, if it includes a detailed
   agenda or is attached to material to be discussed, you
   will want to take it to the meeting, in which case it
   should go into your "Future" ("Tickler") file.
4. Decide now (not later) whether or not you will answer
   the questionnaire. If not, it goes into the wastebasket.
   If you plan to answer it, do so immediately and place

it in your "Out" basket in keeping with the principle of handling each piece of paper only once.

5. This might be put into a "Future" file for the date on which the report is to be prepared, or into a "Subject" file that will be brought out on that date. In the meantime it should be kept out of sight.

6. Leave the letter in the middle of your desk while you make those calls so that you can dictate your answer and complete the action before going on to something else. Of course, if you have to hold the letter for callbacks, you should have a "Pending" file or drawer where it can be put out of sight.

7. Enter the new information in your personal phone directory and throw away the original. Or if the information concerns others in the organization, circulate the notice to them.

8. Send the reports immediately with a buck slip (or jot a note on the original). The thing to avoid on routine matters like this is dictating a formal transmittal memo, creating additional paperwork.

9. If you are not sure, drop it in the wastebasket or pass it along to someone who may be in a better position to judge its value. Don't let it float on your desk because of indecision.

10. If you have a dictating machine, you should dictate your reply immediately. If you use a stenographer, you probably will want to place this in a pile of correspondence to be dictated at a later time. Another possibility, and one well worth considering, is to avoid a written reply and answer by phone, noting the conversation on the letter itself and then sending it to the files.

11. If it is really worth keeping, it should be placed immediately in the personnel file or given to the person who does the filing. But if it is something of a trivial or general nature, make a mental note of the contents and throw it away, keeping in mind that should you need a copy someday, you could obtain one from the sender's files.

12. You should have a system that routinely will bring to

your attention those things you want to consider at future times. It should be on a calendar basis rather than by subject so that you won't have to remember to find the file. Either an accordion file with dates or a time management computer program will accomplish this.

In addition to analyzing paperwork in terms of whether or not a clear routine exists, it is important to analyze it in relation to the principle of delegation. For example, several of the items in the quiz clearly should be handled by a secretary or an assistant if you have one. When going over your answers, consider whether you are the logical person to handle each item.

Parkinson's Law

Professor Parkinson was right: Work expands to fill the time available for its completion. Thus, if you must have a particular task done by three o'clock this afternoon, it is usually done by three o'clock, but if you are given until the end of next month to do the same task, it will take until the end of next month to finish it.

The answer to Parkinson's Law would seem obvious: Make less time available for a given task, and you will get it done more quickly.

Here is where your daily time plan comes in. Without one, you will tend to dawdle at difficult tasks (or even pleasant ones) because you have no deadline. When you think in terms of the task instead of in terms of the time available for it, the sin of perfectionism sets in. You can always put one or two more finishing touches on the job and can con yourself into chalking these up to excellence when in reality you should chalk them up to wheel-spinning.

The only way to overcome this is to work Parkinson's principle in reverse: Set a deadline for each task and hold to that deadline.

Perfectionism

There is a difference between striving for excellence and striving for perfection. The first is attainable, gratifying, and healthy. The second is unattainable, frustrating, and neurotic.

It's also a terrible waste of time.

Workers who make a fetish of perfection are wasting time and money that could be allocated better elsewhere. In inventory taking, for example, all major items should be accounted for, but a system of "sensible approximation" for some of the minor ones makes more sense, because, as someone has pointed out, "The price of perfection is prohibitive."

A stenographer who retypes a lengthy letter because of a trivial error that could be corrected in ink, or a boss who demands that such a letter be retyped, might profit from examining the Declaration of Independence in the National Archives and noting that the inscriber of the document made two errors of omission in copying the final version. Instead of starting over, he inserted the missing letters between the lines with the aid of a caret. If such treatment is acceptable in the case of the document that gave birth to American freedom, surely it also would be acceptable in the case of a letter that is going to be accorded a brief glance en route to someone's file cabinet or wastebasket!

We must stop thinking in terms of absolutes and recognize the price we pay for being unwilling to settle for anything less than perfection. Gail Sheehy put it this way: "Would that there were an award for people who come to understand the concept of enough. Good enough. Successful enough. Thin enough. Rich enough. Socially responsible enough."[1]

When you've done a job well enough, move on to something

else; don't spend more time trying to nitpick your way to perfection. I believe it was Michelangelo who said that one of the secrets of art is knowing when to stop.

And don't forget Patton's Law: A good plan today is preferable to a perfect plan tomorrow!

Planning

The first rule of planning is that you can't plan and work at the same time.

Suppose you are going to build a doghouse. You wouldn't buy the lumber and begin sawing wood and then think about how large the doghouse should be. Yet that's exactly how most people go about their daily activities: They plan as they go along. And then they wonder why "there aren't enough hours in the day"! It's because everything they do takes longer than it should as a result of their failure to do the necessary preliminary planning.

No use of time gives as much "bang for the buck" as planning. Five minutes of careful planning today might save you five hours next week. And yet when people get busy, the first thing they eliminate is planning, because planning is never urgent. Just important.

Always separate planning time from execution time. Thus, instead of planning the day's activities first thing in the morning, plan the preceding afternoon, when you will be more objective. And in planning a project do the planning well in advance of the time when you expect to begin. Then it's almost as if you were planning for someone else, and you give yourself the tough assignments that you'll be tempted to skip if you combine planning and doing.

Plan your days, plan your weeks, plan your projects. And do it on paper. In planning your days and weeks you don't need to worry about details. Ask yourself what are the *major* things you want to accomplish, and block out time for them.

In planning projects, however, do plan in detail and give yourself a deadline on each phase of the project.

Remember, you haven't "planned" to do a thing until you've decided when you're going to do it!

Priorities

There are two ways to set priorities: according to urgency or according to importance.

Most people set them according to urgency, which is why they spend so much time putting out fires and never get started on a project until the deadline is staring them in the face.

If you set priorities according to urgency, you probably have three categories, such as:

1. Must be done today
2. Should be done today, if possible
3. Should be done sometime, but there's no hurry

Suppose you are ready to make out your income-tax return using this system, and it's January 31. Obviously the task would not go in the first category because you have two and a half months before it is due. It could be put in the second category but probably won't be because there is no urgency. Too often it will go into the third category and won't get under way until the deadline is very near. At that point you will find it difficult to find expert help and will be unable to do as thorough a job as you would like.* You mentally kick yourself and promise to start earlier next year. But you won't, because next year the same rationale will apply.

*I am assuming, of course, that you know you don't have a refund coming. People who anticipate a refund somehow select January as a good month to work on tax returns.

I prefer to set priorities first in terms of importance, with urgency a secondary, though significant, consideration.* This involves taking your list of things to do and examining each item first in light of the question "Does this task clearly contribute to the achievement of my lifetime goals or my short-range objectives?" If it does, put a star by it. Then number the starred items in the order in which you would like to do them, taking into account two factors: urgency and the time/benefit ratio.

The time/benefit ratio is simply a way of recognizing that even though one task may be less important than another and may lack urgency, there may be good reason to do it first if the benefit is substantial and the amount of time involved is small. For example, your most important task of the day might be the preparation of a report, which will take most of your day. But suppose you have a couple of minor tasks you can delegate. The few minutes you take (before starting your report) to assign the tasks gives hours more lead time to those doing them. That obviously makes sense.

After you have ranked your starred items by priority, do so with your less important items, then try to accomplish everything in order. You will have a game plan, and your day will be much more productive than if you had to stop to establish priorities each time you were ready to begin a new task.

Procrastination

If *procrastination* is your problem, don't put off doing something about it!

You can't count on sheer willpower to help you overcome this problem. You must have in mind some specific techniques

---

*Obviously, if something is both important *and* urgent, it will get top priority with either system.

that can be brought into play whenever you catch yourself putting off something that shouldn't be put off. Here are some of the most effective techniques.*

THE "SALAMI TECHNIQUE"

An uncut salami is ugly, unwieldy, and unappetizing. But cut it into thin slices, and you transform it into something quite different. Now you have something manageable, something you can "get your teeth into."

It's the same with a big unpleasant task: When you look at it as a whole, it's overwhelming, but when you break it down into small "instant tasks," you change its nature entirely. But the secret is to do it on paper.

Even when the unpleasant task is a small one, this works. For example, suppose you have been putting off an unpleasant phone call. The "salami slices" in this situation might be the following:

1. Look up the phone number and write it down.
2. Set a time to make the call. (Making it immediately calls for more willpower than you apparently have, so let yourself off the hook in return for a firm commitment to make it at a specific time, which you note on your appointment calendar.)
3. Get out the file and review what has happened.
4. Decide precisely what you intend to say.
5. Place the call.

If the task happens to be a major one, the number of "slices" may be quite large, so make a long list. The key is to make each incremental task so simple and quick that by itself it doesn't amount to much. If possible, make it something that can be finished in several minutes. And then, whenever you have a

*For a more extensive discussion of this problem see *Doing It Now: A 12-Step Program for Curing Procrastination and Achieving Your Goals* by Edwin C. Bliss (New York: Charles Scribner's Sons, 1983).

few minutes to spare between appointments or while waiting for a phone call, knock off one of your "instant" tasks. Without such a list of items you may never get started.

Remember, the first slice—the first instant task—is always to list *in writing* the small steps involved in getting the job done.

A variation of this technique is to divide your *time* into small, manageable bits. No matter how unpleasant a task is, you can work on it for just five minutes, so promise yourself that that's all you'll do right now. At the end of five minutes you'll have made inroads on it and will have broken the mental logjam that prevented you from starting, so it will be easy to get back into it. (Many times you'll find you won't *want* to stop; you'll have so much momentum that you'll just keep going.)

So whether it's the task or your time that you divide into increments, remember that the "divide and conquer" principle applies to things you're putting off as much as to military strategy.

THE BALANCE SHEET METHOD

Another good way of getting yourself off dead center is to analyze, in writing, what you are doing.

On the left side of a sheet of paper make a list of all the reasons you are procrastinating on a particular task. On the right side list all the benefits that will accrue if you go ahead and get the job done.

The effect is striking. On the left side you will usually have only one or two pathetic excuses, such as, "It might involve an awkward confrontation" or "I might be bored." On the other side you will find a long list of benefits, the first of which usually is the feeling of relief that comes with getting a necessary but unpleasant task behind you.

The effect of this technique is often swift and dramatic. You awake from your lethargy and begin working to achieve the benefits you have listed.

THE "WORST FIRST" APPROACH

Instead of easing into a task, sometimes your best bet is to do exactly the opposite: Identify the most unpleasant aspect of the task and take care of that first.

For example, suppose you must call a list of ten people to ask for donations to a cause you are involved in, and suppose that there is one person on the list whom you don't like and who is almost sure to turn you down. You dread making the calls mainly because of that person. So start with that person, and whether you're turned down or not, you can then tell yourself that the worst is behind you and from here on it is going to be a breeze.

It's the old principle of eating your spinach first and your cake second. Reverse the order and it doesn't work so well.

Postponing an unpleasant task never makes it more palatable; indeed, the thing becomes harder to do as time goes on. So as someone (I believe it was Mark Twain) said, "If you have to swallow a frog, don't look at it too long. And if you have to swallow *two* frogs, don't swallow the smaller one first!"

HABIT CHANGE: A SYSTEMATIC APPROACH

The final (and most fundamental) approach recognizes that when we fail to act as promptly as we should, it usually is not because the particular task in question is extremely difficult but because we have formed a habit of procrastinating whenever possible. Procrastination is seldom related to just a single item; it is usually an ingrained behavior pattern. If we can change our thinking habits, we can make the previous two methods unnecessary.

The importance of this fact cannot be overemphasized. I am convinced that the most significant difference between effective and ineffective people is that the ineffective person habitually thinks, "This task must be done, but it is unpleasant; therefore, I will put it off as long as I can," whereas the effective person habitually thinks, "This task is unpleasant, but it must be done; therefore, I will do it now so I can forget about it."

But the prospect of changing a deeply rooted habit dismays many people. They've tried it many times through sheer will-power—the New Year's resolution approach—and have failed. It isn't all that difficult, though, provided you use the right system.

William James, the father of American psychology, discussed such a system in his famous essay on habit, which was published in *Popular Science* magazine in 1887 and which subsequently has been validated by the studies of behavioral scientists. As applied to changing the procrastination habit, it would work as follows:

1. Decide to start making the change immediately, as soon as you finish reading this section, while you are motivated. Taking that first step promptly is important.

2. Don't try to do too much too quickly. Instead of trying to revolutionize your entire approach, just force yourself right now to do one thing you have been putting off. Then, beginning tomorrow morning, start each day by doing the most unpleasant thing on your "To Do" list. In other words, apply the "Worst First" system to your daily list of chores.

   Notice that I did not recommend you begin your day with the most *important* thing on your list. The most important things should be allocated specific blocks of time. The most unpleasant thing very often will be a small matter: an overdue apology you've been meaning to make; a confrontation with a fellow worker that you've been putting off; an annoying chore you know you should tackle. Whatever it is, do it before you open the mail, before you return the phone calls left over from the previous afternoon, before you begin your usual morning routine.

   This simple procedure can well set the tone for your entire day. You will get a feeling of exhilaration from knowing that although the day is only fifteen minutes old, you have already accomplished the most unpleasant thing you have to do all day. After you have done this a few days, you will become locked into the habit for life because it is what the behaviorists call a self-reinforcing action—one that has an intrinsic reward that reinforces the behavior. (This is the way an infant learns to stand; the feeling of achievement the baby gets from standing reinforces the actions that were necessary to accomplish the feat the first time, and the procedure soon becomes second nature. Similarly, the "do-it-now" habit can become second nature.)

Although I have recommended that you force yourself to follow this procedure only once a day, you will find that soon it influences decisions throughout the day. Every time you are given an unpleasant chore you will itch to get at it so that you can get that euphoric feeling that comes from promptly disposing of a nasty task.

The beautiful thing about this system is that you don't have to do anything you weren't going to do anyway; you intended to do that chore or you wouldn't have put it on your list. It simply means making it number one on the list instead of number five or ten.

3. There is one caution: During the period when your new habit is taking root, especially during the first couple of weeks, you must be especially careful not to permit any exceptions. William James compared it to rolling up a ball of string: A single slip can undo more than many turns can wind up. Be tough with yourself, just for the first few minutes of the day, each day for the next two weeks, and I can promise you a new habit of priceless value.

So set this aside and start. Now.

Protecting Prime Time

If *you are* an office worker, there are far greater peaks and valleys in your achievement level than there are for manual workers. Chances are, most of your work gets done in only a portion of your working day, the time we might designate prime time.

For most people the first couple of hours of the day are prime time. But many of us ignore this fact and spend those hours doing routine tasks: reading the morning mail (which seldom contains top-priority items), reading periodicals, glancing through the morning newspaper, making routine phone calls, and so on. It doesn't take much thought to see the waste this entails; the best time of the day should be spent on the things that matter most, the things that require top energy, complete alertness, greatest creativity. So schedule your one or two highest payoff tasks for prime time and do the less important ones when you can. (This is the opposite of what most people do, which is to devote their prime time to the most *urgent* task or to squander it on whatever happens to be in front of them at the moment.)

Now that you've chosen your priorities and scheduled them for the most productive part of your day, the next step is to get people to leave you alone long enough to get them done. The things we discussed under "Interruptions" can help, but in the next section we will look at another technique that many people have found useful—the "Quiet Time" concept.

Quiet Time

Quiet time. The very phrase is soothing, conjuring up a picture of calm and tranquility. But in today's busy world it seems unattainable, especially during working hours.

It isn't unattainable. The only question is whether you are willing to pay the price for it.

To get quiet time you have to carve out a chunk of your day when you simply won't permit routine interruptions. "But that won't work in my case," you say. "I have to deal with the public, I have a demanding boss, I have a telephone, I have crises to deal with. . . ."

That's true. It's also true of everybody else, yet some people do manage to set aside a portion of their day to concentrate on some important task without fear of interruption. And they are the ones who are most effective because creative thinking is difficult or impossible amid constant annoying distractions.

One way of doing this is the Quiet Hour. Designate one hour during which everyone in the organization leaves everyone else alone except in case of an emergency. During that period all phone calls are screened, and the caller is told, "Yes, she is in, but she's busy right now. Could I have her call you back?" If the caller pleads urgency, the call is put through; otherwise, the message is taken. It helps, of course, if people outside the organization have been forewarned: "We have a Quiet Hour between ten and eleven, so from now on you'll find I'm easier to reach if you'll call before ten or after eleven. But if you need to reach me during that hour, just tell them it's urgent and they'll put you through."

That doesn't offend people; on the contrary, it flatters them. In effect you're saying, "We have this system to minimize interruptions, but you're so important that I want to make sure you know how to get around the system whenever you need to." People won't abuse it: Who wants to call someone at the one time of day that person has indicated he or she doesn't want to be interrupted?

The Quiet Hour idea will meet with opposition at first. It's best to present it as an experiment and get suggestions from the people involved as to the best time for the Quiet Hour. If they have some input and if they realize that the concept isn't going to be forced upon them, they will cooperate.

But you will need some way of reminding people about the Quiet Hour. One insurance company that has a quiet hour from 8 to 9 A.M. makes an announcement over the public address system at 8 A.M. sharp: "Good morning." That's all it takes to remind everyone, from the president on down, to end all conversation and idle chatter and get down to business.[1] In some organizations the words QUIET HOUR appear automatically on everyone's computer screen at the appropriate time. One company has QUIET HOUR posters put up on each department's bulletin board at the appropriate time each day, and anyone who forgets and interrupts anyone else during that hour with a nonurgent matter is responsible for putting up and taking down the posters until someone else goofs.

If your organization doesn't want to try the Quiet Hour, you might want to do it on an individual basis. Tell your co-workers that since you have a one-track mind, you've decided to protect a period of your day from interruption. Ask for their cooperation. They'll promise to comply—but they'll promptly forget, and you'll have to remind them several times before they understand that you really mean business. Once you've established the practice as a habit, you'll be surprised at the difference it makes. One executive describes her Quiet Hour as an "emotional foxhole" in the day.

Another technique is to set aside a longer period of time but only once a week. Some executives, for example, block out one morning a week as their quiet time. (Wednesday morning seems to be the most popular choice.) The New Business Department at Northwestern Mutual Life Insurance Company has gone a step further, setting aside an entire day. Every Wednesday the phones are turned off so that the underwriters can do their work instead of answering questions from the field. The policy has been in effect since 1984, with dramatic results: as much as a 50 percent increase in productivity.

Northwestern, incidentally, has a longstanding commitment to the concept of quiet, having billed itself for many years as "the quiet company." Donald J. Schuenke, president of the company, commissioned a study to examine the use of quiet in business. The study was made by six researchers over a period of eighteen months, including participation by a number of America's top corporate chief executives. It indicated that without the respite provided by periodic quiet time, executives have less sense of control over their lives and are more prone to emotional exhaustion and burnout.[2]

In planning your day, then, begin by scheduling some time for quiet concentration. You'll be doing yourself and your organization a favor.

Radical Surgery

Time-wasting activities are like cancers. They serve no useful function, they drain off vitality, they never disappear of their own accord, and they have a tendency to grow.

The only cure is radical surgery. If you are wasting time in volunteer groups that you don't believe in or in social activities that are a bore or in office practices that divert you from your department's real goals, face up to the fact that these things are sapping your time and energy, and do whatever needs to be done to cut them out, once and for all.

Robert Townsend suggests that every company should have a vice president in charge of killing things. He says, "General Foods, the AFL-CIO, the Bureau of the Budget, and the Ford Foundation should make it a practice to wipe out their worst product, service, or activity every so often. And I don't mean cutting it back or remodeling it—I mean right between the eyes."[1]

You also must perform radical surgery on your daily "To Do" list, which nearly always contains one or two tasks that y̶o̶u̶ ̶w̶o̶u̶l̶d̶ ̶l̶i̶k̶e̶ to do or that someone has *asked* you to do but which simply take more time than they're worth. Although we may identify other tasks as our "priorities," we leave these also-rans on the list despite the fact that we can't or shouldn't do them. Get rid of them. They are what Peter Drucker calls "posteriorities." He says, "The job is, however, not to set priorities. That is easy. Everybody can do it. The reason why so few executives concentrate is the difficulty of setting 'posteriorities'—that is, deciding what tasks not to tackle—and of sticking to the decision."[2]

It isn't easy because we all have a lot of "back burner" tasks we'd like to undertake if only we could find time for them. But time is never "found"; it is carved out of a busy day, and you won't (or shouldn't) carve out time for these low-priority tasks. Consequently, they remain on your list indefinitely, creating guilt. Or you give in to the temptation to do them instead of an admittedly higher payoff task that is less pleasant. Either way, you lose.

Check your time log, your appointment calendar, your extra-curricular activities, your reading list, your television viewing habits, and ask if each activity is so important or so satisfying that it's worth making time for. If not, give it the ax.

Self-Quiz

If you want to get an idea of how effectively you are managing your own time, give yourself the following quiz:

	Yes	No
1. Do I have—in writing—a clearly defined set of lifetime goals?	☐	☐
2. Do I have a similar set of goals for the next six months?	☐	☐
3. Have I done something today to move me closer to my lifetime goals? My short-term goals?	☐	☐

4. Do I have a clear idea of what I want to accomplish at work during the coming week? □ □

5. Do I try to do the most important tasks during my prime time? □ □

6. Do I concentrate on objectives instead of procedures, judging myself by accomplishment instead of by amount of activity? □ □

7. Do I set priorities according to importance, not urgency? □ □

8. Do I make constructive use of commute time? □ □

9. Do I delegate as much work as possible? □ □

10. Do I delegate challenging jobs as well as routine ones? □ □

11. Do I delegate authority along with responsibility? □ □

12. Do I prevent subordinates from delegating upward those decisions and tasks that they find difficult or worrisome? □ □

13. Do I effectively use the aid of subordinates to get better control of my time? □ □

14. Have I taken steps to prevent unneeded information and publications from reaching my desk and intruding on my time? □ □

15. When debating whether to file something, do I follow the principle "If in doubt, throw it out"? □ □

16. In meetings do I try to crystallize what the issues are and summarize the decisions made and responsibilities assigned? □ □

17. Do I try to handle matters by phone or in person whenever I have a choice, using written communication only when it is clearly indicated?

18. Do I try to put work out of my mind when away from the office, except in clear emergencies?

19. Do I force myself to make minor decisions quickly?

20. Am I on guard against the recurring crisis, taking steps to make sure that it won't occur again?

21. Do I always set deadlines for myself and others?

22. Do I force myself to take time to plan?

23. Have I discontinued any unprofitable routines or activities recently?

24. Do I keep things in my pocket or briefcase that I can work on whenever I get spare moments: in lines, waiting rooms, trains, planes?

25. Do I try to live in the present, thinking in terms of what needs to be done now instead of rehashing past errors or successes or worrying about the future?

26. Do I make periodic use of a time log to determine whether I am slipping back into unproductive routines?

27. Am I continually striving to establish habits that will make me more effective?

28. Do I keep in mind the dollar value of my time?

29. Do I leverage my time by mak-

ing time for high-payoff tasks, even
though they may lack urgency?   □   □
30. Am I really in control of my
time? Are my actions determined
primarily by me, not by circumstances or by other people's priori-
ties?   □   □

Give yourself this quiz every six months. If any of your
answers are no, review the appropriate section and determine
what you can do to correct the deficiency. The price of effective time use is eternal vigilance, and the rewards are well
worth it.

Sleep

Can you afford to spend one third of your life unconscious?
On the other hand, from a health standpoint can you afford
not to? How much sleep do you really need?

It depends.

Sleep needs vary widely. According to the Better Sleep
Council, "Normal sleep times range from five to ten hours; the
average is seven and a half. About one or two people in one
hundred can get by with just five hours; another small minor-
ity needs twice that amount."[1]

Many well-known people have had very short sleep spans.
Among notables who have done well on only four hours a
night (or even less) are Thomas Edison, Napoleon, John D.
MacArthur, Buckminster Fuller, Pope Leo XIII, Aristotle
Onassis, Lyndon Johnson, and Charles Darwin.

But some have required more than the average. Einstein,
for example, required ten hours a night.

Although getting more sleep than you need produces no
benefits, it's better to err on the side of more sleep than less.
Two leading sleep authorities, Dr. William C. Dement of Stanford and Dr. James B. Maas of Cornell, estimate that about 100

million Americans are chronically sleepy in the daytime, and they note that drowsiness in the daytime generally indicates a less-than-optimal amount of deep and continuous sleep at night.

In a study at Detroit's Henry Ford Hospital, sleep researchers found that healthy people who slept just one additional hour felt better, became more alert, and performed better on the job. In many cases additional nighttime sleep eliminates the afternoon lethargy that many people blame on lunch, but which actually is caused by a sleep deficit.

But some people would do better with *less* sleep. "Since too much time in bed can make some people feel sluggish, don't assume that more is always better," is the advice of the Better Sleep Council. "Listen to your body's signals and adjust your sleep schedule to suit them."[2]

Experimentation is the only way to determine your optimum amount of sleep. Pay attention to when drowsiness occurs at night. For most people sleepiness is negligible during much of the evening and then rapidly increases. This period of rapid change should precede your bedtime. How you feel during the day is also an important indicator—but it is important that it be measured not against how much sleep you had the previous night, but how much you've been getting over the preceding *several* nights.

Sounds like a lot of trouble, but it's worth it. If you find you are now getting less than your optimum, it will pay you to eliminate late-night television; you'll feel better and you'll get more done during the day. On the other hand, if you're now getting more sleep than you need and you cut back, the payoff could be considerable. An hour less sleep would give you a chance to do a lot of those things you've been meaning to do but couldn't because "there aren't enough hours in the day!"*

*For more information on sleep, contact the Association of Professional Sleep Societies, 604 Second Street, S.W., Rochester, MN 55901.

Speed Reading

If *your problem* is that you spend too much time reading, a rapid-reading course won't solve it. The solution is to read more selectively.

It is true that some people have bad reading habits such as subvocalizing or rereading phrases unnecessarily. A reading course can help break those patterns and increase speed somewhat, but a surprising number of students who make some progress in increasing reading speed report that after a few months they slip back into their old patterns. And as for the claim that some people can read forty thousand words per minute (which is the equivalent of reading *Gone with the Wind* in twelve minutes) and still comprehend what they are reading, consider the results of a test made at a major university. A pair of speed-reading-course graduates read an article in which lines from another essay had been interspersed. They were unaware that what they were reading was nonsense until it was pointed out by another student who had not taken the speed-reading course.

Perhaps the most succinct comment on selectivity in reading is by James McCay, who asks, "Would you like to be able to read fifty thousand words a minute? There are many times

when it is easy to do this if you know how. All you have to be able to do is recognize within one minute that a fifty thousand-word book does not suit your purposes and decide *not* to read it."[1]

It is difficult to resist the lure of reading, especially when there is something less pleasant that you should be doing. Keep in mind these words of the British critic F. L. Lucas: "It is mere common sense never to undertake a piece of work or read a book without asking, 'Is it worth the amount of life it will cost?'"

That simple question can save you more time than all the speed-reading courses ever devised.

Stand-up Desk

The Declaration of Independence was written at Thomas Jefferson's stand-up desk. Thomas Wolfe, who was very tall, used the top of a refrigerator as a desk. Other writers who did all or much of their work standing up include Ernest Hemingway, Lewis Carroll, Virginia Woolf, Vladimir Nabokov, and Winston Churchill. (And while I hesitate to place myself in such distinguished company, I might note that this book is being written mostly at a stand-up desk.)

Among noted executives who have helped popularize the stand up desk in recent years are John Opel of IBM, C. Peter McColough and David T. Kearns of Xerox, William LaMothe of Kellogg Company, Donald Rumsfeld of G. D. Searle & Company, Robert A. Beck of Prudential Insurance Company, Fletcher Byrom of Koppers Corporation, John Beckett of Transamerica Corporation, and Preston Martin of the Federal Reserve Board.

People who work standing up are often passionate advocates of the practice. For some, their "pulpit" is their only desk, in which case a tall stool is usually kept nearby for occasional use. More commonly, the stand-up desk is used in conjunction with a regular one, providing an opportunity to switch between the two working levels to reduce fatigue.

People can think more rapidly when standing. A study made at the University of Southern California[1] indicated that the brain's information-processing speed accelerates from 5 to 20 percent when a person is standing instead of sitting. "Standing up improves reaction time, particularly for the elderly and relatively unfit individuals, and for everyone working on difficult tasks," says Dr. Max Vercruyssen, who directed the study. "Our data suggest that simply standing up causes a heart rate increase of about ten beats per minute and an increase in neural stimulation, resulting in improved cognitive functions."

You don't need to invest in custom-built furniture to get this benefit. If you have a counter in your work area, make generous use of it. A makeshift arrangement, such as a portable lectern sitting on a table, can provide an elbow-height work area, which is the ideal.

One final word: If you work standing for long periods, you should have a stool with rungs or some other arrangement that permits you to put your weight on one foot and get the other one off the floor, reducing back strain. As one back expert has noted, saloonkeepers know the importance of this: "A bar rail relaxes customers, and relaxed customers are likely to linger longer and to order another drink."

I'll drink to that. Standing up.

Subordinates' Time

If you have one or more subordinates, chances are they consider you an obstacle to efficient use of their time. Every list of time problems I have seen includes "interruptions by boss" or "boss-imposed busy work" or "indecision by boss." Your subordinates may be too polite or too timid to tell you so, but take my word for it, you cause time problems for the people who report to you. And because your success is linked to their output and their morale, you pay a high price for it.

A little humility can help here. Make it clear to subordinates that you understand their work sometimes can be more urgent than yours and that in case of conflict they should use their own good judgment or at least discuss the situation with you instead of automatically giving top priority to any request that happens to originate from On High.

Encourage subordinates to think about time use and to level with you whenever you ask them to do things they consider wasteful or inefficient. Ask them for suggestions that will help you make better use of your own time.

Also, urge your staff to keep a time log, but not unless you have done it yourself or they will resent the implication that you consider yourself blessed with omniscience. (And as a matter of fact, you need effective time management techniques even more than those under you because [1] your failures or successes tend to be magnified more because of your exalted status, and [2] the higher you rise in a hierarchy, the more discretionary time you have, with correspondingly more time-use decisions to be made.)

Encourage subordinates to think in terms of "managing the boss." Let them know that you recognize the degree to which their actions can control your time, and respect their time so they will respect yours.

Technophobia

The complexity of computer-age gadgetry, and the arcane vocabulary one must learn even to discuss it, is a turnoff for many people. They would rather continue doing things the old-fashioned pre-microchip way than confront the electronic dragon.

That's a shame because they are going to be left in the dust. The twenty-first century will have no mercy on those companies—or individuals—who don't capitalize fully on the miracles of modern electronics.

Of course, the mere fact that something is "high tech"

doesn't mean you should use it. For people who don't have to
juggle a lot of tasks with conflicting time pressures, whose
lives are relatively simple, the quickest way for them to do
their planning and scheduling may still be pencil and paper.
But for most people that isn't true. Technology has revolution-
ized the way we do things in the "information age," and those
who understand and utilize the latest developments can leverage their time and efforts to an incredible degree.*

But change comes slowly for many people, particularly
those who are not *required* to use a computer. As of this writing, 45 percent of top executives have personal computers in
their offices. Of these, 69 percent use their PCs regularly, but
only 39 percent consider themselves very proficient at using
them.[1]

Just getting a computer system installed doesn't move you
into the information age. If you use your system for only a few
obvious functions such as mailing lists and word processing,
you may be overlooking capabilities that could save you a lot
of time and money.

An example of a company that has exploited the power of
the computer is Mrs. Fields, Inc., the world's largest retailer
of cookies and specialty bakery products. Randy Fields, chairman of the company, considers it his most valuable tool for
organizing ideas, managing people, tracking assignments,
handling routine decision-making, doing routine paperwork,
and communicating between branch offices and headquarters
at Park City, Utah. He says his most essential business tool is
a laptop computer, which he claims is never more than ten
feet away no matter where he is. And he emphasizes that the
use of technology must begin at the top. "The example must
come from the CEO," he says. "You must be a computer user.
Learn to type. Use a keyboard. If you don't learn at some
point, you'll be a dinosaur."[2]

The most common mistake computer users make is to learn
how to use the computer for only one or two narrow purposes,

---

*For a list of some companies that produce time management software see
page 132.

never getting around to exploring the computer's potential. After you have mastered the basics, make the excellent investment of a few dollars to take an advanced class. Better still, hire a tutor to spend two or three hours with you going over some of the functions and shortcuts you don't know. Whatever your job, it's a good bet that your computer can save you lots of time, and it doesn't make sense to say that you "don't have the time" to find out how!

Tempo

After waiting eleven months for the army to reply to her inquiry about a study of Rocky Mountain Arsenal workers exposed to nerve gas, Congresswoman Pat Schroeder of Denver sent her "First Annual Dilatory Conduct Award" (a twelve-ounce jar of Br'er Rabbit molasses) to the army's legislative liaison office.

If your organization is in the competition for such an award, ask what you can do to step up the tempo of activity and to stimulate a little wholesome impatience.

Massachusetts management consultant Charles H. Ford notes that "the tempo of a company—the speed with which it moves, makes and implements decisions, identifies and solves problems, grasps opportunities, reacts to competitive pressures, or adapts to abrupt changes in marketing patterns and business climates—is something to which most executives and corporate bodies remain blissfully indifferent."[1] And yet, he suggests, it is often the one factor that contributes most to corporate success or lack of it.

Tempo is a reflection of the attitude of the person in charge. If that person is goal-oriented ("Now that we know exactly what our objective is, let's do whatever has to be done to get there"), the pace is brisk. If that person is procedure-oriented ("Let's make sure we follow directives to the letter, and don't risk any mistakes"), the pace is sluggish.

The same thing is true at a personal level. If you are daw-dling, drifting, and *working at* a task instead of *doing* it, blow the whistle on yourself and answer these questions:

1. Exactly why am I trying to do this task? Is it really worthwhile? If so—
2. Have I set a deadline for myself? Have I resolved to meet it?
3. If my life depended upon doing the task in half the time I have allocated, what shortcuts would I take? Is there really any reason *not* to take them?

To quote Charles Ford again, "The key is controlled ur-gency, treating every matter as something urgent to get done and out of the way. It means less time spent on useless conver-sation, less waiting patiently for someone else to move before you do, more action rather than putting things aside for later (whenever that is)."

Tension and Time Use

There is a common belief that tension is bad, that quiet and tranquility are the goals for which we should strive.

Nonsense. Without tension nothing gets done. Quiet and contentment are desirable (in fact, a daily period of medita-tion is an excellent use of time), but there must be alternating periods of tension or you can slip into lethargy. What keeps a watch going is the tension on the mainspring.

Positive tension can take many forms: a deadline that must be met, an awareness that your work is going to be judged, a sense of competition with others. These pressures bring out the best in people, challenging them to use time as effectively as possible. Good management involves building a reasonable amount of positive tension into your relationships with subor-dinates, and good self-management involves finding ways to put some pressure on yourself to perform. Making a public commitment to undertake a job on which you have been procrastinating, for example, is one way of putting pressure on yourself.

There is a kind of tension that is bad, of course, the kind that produces harmful stress. Tension headaches and other ailments associated with stress are often a result of frustration growing out of poor time management practices: failure to set priorities, failure to plan ahead, failure to concentrate on a single item at a time, failure to delegate properly, indecision, failure to schedule periods of quiet time when you can tackle top-priority jobs without interruption. If bad habits are causing you undue stress, read the appropriate entry in this book, do what it says, and relax!

Tidbits of Time

When the person you were supposed to meet for lunch is late or when your car isn't ready at the shop as promised or when you have to stand in a slow line at the bank—don't write these moments off as lost time! Consider them instead as windfall moments you can use to do something that otherwise would have to wait.

When you are stranded for an hour in an airport between planes, for example, why spend that hour in the bar drinking beer and stewing and staring at a television set? Why not take a brisk walk around the airport?

Salespeople often find that the time spent in a reception room awaiting an interview is enough to catch up on all their paperwork: writing a call report about the preceding contact, writing notes to customers and prospects, planning future calls, updating expense accounts, and so on. Anyone can find appropriate small tasks that can be done in spare moments; it's just a matter of having the necessary forms or materials on hand.

If you travel frequently, for example, it is helpful to keep a "travel kit" of materials that you might find useful on a plane or while waiting for someone. Mine includes a few envelopes, stationery, stamps, pen, Hi-liter, pocket recorder, blank tapes, calculator, address book, and three-by-five cards for jotting down notes. I also will have with me some magazines or a book from my reading pile, and my earphone cassette tape player and a few cassettes—usually a mix of instructional or motivational tapes and some of my favorite music. Thus prepared, instead of dreading the possibility of my flight being late, I almost hope that it will be, giving me an opportunity to get to some of those things that otherwise would never get done.

Be prepared to exploit those tidbits of time that fate hands you, remembering that if somebody keeps you waiting, it's your fault, not theirs, if your time is wasted.

Time, Dollar Value Of

P*eople who are paid* by the hour are much more aware of the value of time than are salaried workers. (If you don't believe this, try getting a psychiatrist or a plumber to take an hour off during the day to discuss some minor matter.)

So for purposes of time management, consider that you are being paid by the hour, whether you actually are or not. To find your rate, take your annual salary in thousands of dollars and divide by two, and that is roughly your hourly pay.

For example, if you make $32,000 a year, you are getting about $16 an hour. When a co-worker prolongs a visit by fifteen minutes to exchange a bit of gossip, the dollar value of the time you've lost is $4. People who would cringe at the thought of putting a match to four $1 bills and watching them burn think nothing of watching $4 worth of precious time go up in smoke.

A great woman who understood this principle was Queen Elizabeth I, whose dying words were, "All my possessions for a moment of time!" Remember those words the next time you're tempted to throw away a few precious minutes.

Time for What?

If you follow all the advice in this book, you are going to save yourself a lot of time; my guess is that you will have between one and two extra hours of discretionary time at your disposal each day. So what are you going to do with it? That's an important question because if you're not careful, much of the time you save will get away from you before you know it, and you'll be right back where you started.

Lay claim to the time you save. Plan it. Allocate time to do the fun things you've been wanting to do and to the activities that will move you closer to your personal and professional goals. You've earned those additional hours at considerable effort; make sure you use them well.

Time Log

The time log is the most valuable single tool ever devised for getting control of time. It isn't intended as part of your permanent routine, only as a diagnostic technique to be used every few months or whenever effectiveness seems to be slipping. It's easier than it looks.

Make a chart similar to the one on page 102, adapted to your own situation. Note that it is a double-entry system with two categories: "Activity" (the things you do) and "Business Function" (the purpose for doing them). For each fifteen-minute period during the day you put two check marks on the log, one under each category. And where needed, indicate under "Notes" exactly what you were doing.

Tape the time log to the sliding work shelf you have on your desk so it will be out of sight except when you are using it. Then every half-hour or so (but no less often than each hour),

Time	_ ACTIVITY →										_ BUSINESS FUNCTION →								NOTES
	Reading	Dictation	Paperwork	Phone Calls	Consultations	Meetings	Inspections	Travel	Planning	Other	Sales	Purchasing	Production	Finance	Personnel	Customer Relations	Admin Routine	Other	
7:00- 7:15																			
7:15- 7:30																			
7:30- 7:45																			
7:45- 8:00																			
8:00- 8:15									X									X	CHATTING
8:15- 8:30			X													X	X		INCOMING MAIL
8:30- 8:45	X														X				MAIL
8:45- 9:00				X							X								MISC. PHONE CALLS
9:00- 9:15	X																X		READING NEWSPAPER
9:15- 9:30	X																X		READING TRADE JOURNAL
9:30- 9:45									X	X								X	COFFEE BREAK
9:45-10:00									X	X								X	COFFEE BREAK
10:00-10:15			X											X					ACME - WARRANTY PROBLEM
10:15-10:30					X					X					X				SAW RICHARDSON
10:30-10:45																			
10:45-11:00		X											X						WORK ON SALARY SCHEDULE

TOTAL

11:00-11:15	"
11:15-11:30	WEEKLY REPORT
11:30-11:45	SAW OFFICE MACHINE SALES PERSON
11:45-12:00	LUNCH WITH RICHARDSON
12:00-12:15	"
12:15-12:30	"
12:30-12:45	"
12:45-1:00	"
1:00-1:15	RETURN TO OFFICE
1:15-1:30	RETURNED MISC. PHONE CALLS
1:30-1:45	"
1:45-2:00	MET WITH BOSS
2:00-2:15	"
2:15-2:30	PERSONAL ERRANDS
2:30-2:45	"
2:45-3:00	TRAVEL TO SEE JOHNSON
3:00-3:15	JOHNSON MEETING
3:15-3:30	"
3:30-3:45	RETURN TO OFFICE
3:45-4:00	CHAT WITH ROGERS
4:00-4:15	DICTATION ON SALARY SCHEDULE
4:15-4:30	READ PM NEWSPAPER
4:30-4:45	SAW MURPHY RE NEW PROCEDURES
4:45-5:00	"

bring it up to date. The cumulative time it will take to do this for the entire day will be perhaps three or four minutes. But the results will be astounding.

You will find that you had no idea where your time was really going. Memory is notoriously unreliable in this area because we tend to remember the highlights of the day—the moments when we were accomplishing something—and we overlook the time that was wasted or ineffectively used. The trivial items, the minor distractions, are too unimportant to be remembered. *Yet these are the items we most want to identify!*

After keeping a log for two or three days, you will be struck with the opportunities for improvement. For example, you probably will find you spend far more time than you realized reading trade publications, newspapers, reports, and so on, and will be motivated to find a way to cut down on this activity. You may be surprised at the amount of time spent traveling to appointments and will work to consolidate travel time through better scheduling or through greater use of the phone. You may find that your fifteen-minute coffee break runs more like forty minutes, counting from the time you leave your desk to go to the coffee shop until the time you get back. Maybe it's worth it, but you really can't judge until you see written evidence of exactly how much time is involved.

Most important of all, however, you will be surprised at the small percentage of your time you actually spend on what you would admit are your top-priority items, how little time you spend planning, anticipating problems, exploiting opportunities, and working toward major goals, compared to the amount of time you spend putting out fires and doing routine low-priority tasks. A time log has the same effect as a dash of cold water on your face in the morning; it's a bit unpleasant for a moment, but it wakes you up and gets you started.

It takes a bit of self-discipline to undertake the making and keeping of a time log, but I can promise you that (1) it will take far less time than you would think to keep one for a few days, and (2) it is bound to point you toward important improvements in the way you spend your time. Start one today.

Time Management and Your Heart

In *my time management* seminars I occasionally encounter people whose motivation in attending is not to achieve control and balance in their lives but to find ways of running faster on the treadmill they have created for themselves. They are obsessed with doing more and more things faster and faster. Their motor is already racing, and they want to learn how to squeeze out a few more rpm's.

That isn't time management; it's a neurosis. It's what is now known as Type-A behavior. And I try (often unsuccessfully) to convince these people that the solution to their problem is not to cram more into their lives but to eliminate, to learn how to simplify, prioritize, organize . . . and relax.

Dr. Meyer Friedman, medical director of the Meyer Friedman Institute in San Francisco and one of the co-discoverers of Type-A behavior, says that such behavior has two components: *impatience* (a continuous sense of time urgency) and *anger* (easily aroused hostility about trivial events). "Much of the recent research has emphasized the importance of anger in contributing to a coronary heart attack," he says, "but I believe that impatience continues to play as important a role. Although impatience can serve a purpose, *chronic* impatience is a danger signal and should be dealt with. It is a habit, and habits can be changed."[1] Changing that habit involves, quite simply, doing the things recommended in this book. By practicing sound time management principles you'll not only accomplish more every day but there's a good chance you'll also live longer.

Among the many physical signs of Type-A personalities are:

□ excessive blinking
□ choppy, staccato voice patterns

☐ fist clenching
☐ habitual use of obscene language
☐ tension in the jaw muscles
☐ excessive sweating around the forehead and upper lip
☐ habitually completing other people's sentences

If you recognize those symptoms in your own behavior, take a good look at your life and put into practice that well-known advice of Henry David Thoreau: "Simplify, simplify, simplify."

Some suggestions from Dr. Friedman:

☐ Be confident that you can alter Type-A behavior. It's just a matter of changing some habits.
☐ Rid your life of the events that have no long-term significance.
☐ Refuse to let the trivial errors of others get under your skin. Learn to mentally shrug your shoulders instead of reacting emotionally to minor annoyances.
☐ Get the spiritual element back into your life. Give time and effort to being a better person, not just a better engineer or carpenter or salesperson.
☐ Learn to appreciate the three P's: people, pets, and plants.
☐ Devote some time each day to relaxation. Learn to use deep breathing during the day to relieve stress.
☐ Exercise. Go for the moderate exercises such as walking, biking, golf, gardening.

Another of Dr. Friedman's recommendations may seem facetious, but it isn't: *Learn to enjoy traffic!* He says, "Instead of fuming at every red light, make commuting one of the most productive parts of your day. Do your thinking and planning, listen to music, play learning cassettes . . . have a very compelling talking book along—just for the car—to 'read' when traffic is really bad."[2]

I suspect Dr. Friedman, if asked, would have one further recommendation: Unless it is really essential in your work, get rid of that car phone!

Good time management—the concept of "working smarter, not harder"—can help you cope with Type-A behavior and help you shed such unprofitable habits as perfectionism, wheel-spinning, failure to delegate, inability to set priorities, and going through life without having established realistic goals. This will enable you to find some time each day to devote to what Dr. Friedman calls "things worth being" rather than just "things worth having," time for reading, exercise, meditation, relaxation, solitude, and for social contacts unrelated to business. It can mean a whole new dimension to living. For health as well as happiness, it's worth a try.

Unfinished Business

In baseball, victory is determined not by hits but by runs. The team that gets a runner to third base and no further doesn't get credit for three-quarters of a run.

It's that way with a task. Getting started is fine and carrying it forward is fine, but until the task is completed, you haven't done what you set out to do. Yet many people form the habit of "working for a while" on a project, then setting it aside, kidding themselves into thinking that they have accomplished something. All they are doing is leaving men stranded on base!

This wastes time because (1) often you won't return to the task, so the time spent is lost, or (2) when you do return, you have to take time to build up momentum again, retrace steps, review what was done, and get thoughts and papers in order.

Once you start something, finish it. Don't accumulate a backlog of half-finished projects. In the words of William James, "Nothing is so fatiguing as the eternal hanging on of an uncompleted task."

Of course there will be times when the task is too large to be completed at one time. How do you handle those situations?

Simple. You divide and conquer. Break the task down into small, manageable segments (preferably in writing) and assign yourself to complete action on one segment before stopping. Then, instead of feeling that you are leaving a lot of loose ends when you put the task aside, you will feel that you have completed one phase of the project and are ready to begin the next. (This is essentially the Salami Technique discussed under "Procrastination.")

Suppose, for example, that you have a lengthy report to prepare. Don't think in terms of "working on it for an hour or so." Instead, assign yourself the task of *completing* the outline or *finishing* the research or *writing* the introduction before you stop. Then you will be able to put it aside with a feeling of having accomplished something specific and with a clear idea of what comes next. You will avoid the mental block that results from having loose ends to gather up before you can start again.

People who habitually set tasks aside before finishing them usually do so because of a subconscious desire to feel—and appear—very busy. If instead of finishing an assignment you set it aside when it's partly done and start working on something else, you soon find yourself engaged in a large number of "ongoing" projects. Having so many irons in the fire makes you feel important. The work piles up on your desk, and you get a masochistic satisfaction from being "snowed under" all the time.

You're kidding yourself. You'll feel better about yourself and will impress your co-workers a lot more if you take the opposite tack: Always finish what you start. The mind-set we are talking about here has been described as "the compulsion to closure," and it's one of the great secrets of achievement.

In the words of Napoleon: "When you set out to take Vienna, *take Vienna!*"

Upward Delegation

Delegation involves giving subordinates assignments commensurate with their abilities and their duties, together with the authority to get the job done. Too often the process is reversed, and a subordinate gives the boss back a partially finished job that should have been completed at the lower level. This not only causes the boss to do things that somebody else ought to be doing but also prevents the subordinate from growing. And the subordinate's growth is essential if the boss is to get work done and take on more responsibility.

In a *Harvard Business Review* article, William Oncken, Jr., and Donald L. Wass give a perceptive analysis of what they call "subordinate-imposed time":

Let us imagine that a manager is walking down the hall and that he notices one of his subordinates, Mr. A, coming up the hallway. When they are abreast of one another, Mr. A greets the manager with, "Good morning. By the way, we've got a problem. You see . . ." As Mr. A continues, the manager recognizes in this problem the same two characteristics common to all the problems his subordinates gratuitously bring to his attention; namely, the manager knows (a) enough to get involved, but (b) not enough to make the on-the-spot decision expected of him. Eventually, the manager says, "So glad you brought this up. I'm in a rush right now. Meanwhile, let me think about it, and I'll let you know." Then he and Mr. A part company.

Let us analyze what has just happened. Before the two of them met, on whose back was the "monkey"? The subordinate's. After they parted, on whose back was it? The manager's. Subordinate-imposed time begins the moment a monkey successfully executes a leap from the back of a subordinate to the back of his superior and does not end until the monkey is returned to its proper owner for care and feeding.[1]

The commonest form of upward delegation is the submission of partially completed work by workers who count on their superiors to make the tough decisions or put on the finishing touches or check for possible errors. When a subordinate gets away with this, it is usually because the boss believes that he or she can finish the job easier and faster. This may be true, but the job of the manager is to manage, not to do someone else's work.

The best solution to the problem of upward delegation is a military concept known as the principle of "completed staff work." It is believed that the idea originated with Napoleon, and it is a standard operating procedure in just about every modern army, navy, and air force in the world.

In a military context, the idea is that under no circumstances does the chief of staff go into the commanding general and say, "General, here is the problem we face. What would you like us to do about it?"

Instead, the chief of staff will say something like, "General, here is the problem. As I see it we have the following options available to us. . . ." Then after discussing each of the options and indicating the pros and cons, he might say, "My recommendation is option number three. What do you think?"

Usually the general will approve the recommendation—after all, it's a recommendation from his experts, who have taken the time to analyze the problem and come up with their judgment—or he might overrule them. But whatever he does is done in light of an analysis of the options and *a firm recommendation from his subordinates, which he gets without asking for it.* It's built into the system.

Train your subordinates to provide completed staff work. Say, "My door is always open; I'm available whenever you need help. All I ask is one thing: Any time you bring me a problem, I want you also to bring your opinion as to what you think is the best way of dealing with it. I'll take it from there. I'll even make your decisions for you, if you want, provided you always bring me that recommendation."

Usually they won't bother you because when they've thought it through, they will realize what is clearly the best solution. But sometimes you *are* the one who should make the final decision. At least you can now make it in the light of someone else's analysis and judgment. And it's often true that two heads are better than one.

(If you don't have subordinates, it's still worth complying with this principle even if your boss doesn't require it. Never dump a problem on your boss's desk and say, "Tell me what to do." Always go in with a firm recommendation.)

Incidentally, if subordinates make a habit of leaving all the decisions up to you, it may be because you are forcing them to do so. Ask yourself whether you are giving them the *authority* to do whatever needs to be done. If not, you can't blame them for running back to you with half-solved problems.

User-Friendly Office

S*tand back* from your desk or work station for a moment and look at it objectively. What emotions does it seem to evoke? Are there things about it that annoy you? Is it an easy place to concentrate, or are there unnecessary distractions? Is valuable work space taken up by books, machines, or files that are seldom used? Taken in total, does it convey a feeling of order or disorder?

In other words, are you really *comfortable* with your office or work station (comfortable, that is, not in the sense of its being a place to lounge or relax, but in terms of its being a good place to do your work)?

If you aren't pleased, do something about it. You may have to spend some time or money, but a big part of your life is spent in your office. Your work space should be free of unnecessary stress.

Give particular attention to your chair. Ergonomists—those who specialize in designing things to meet human needs—say that the height of the seat should be adjusted so that the feet rest flat on the floor with the knees bent at a 90-degree angle. The backrest should be adjustable, of course, and should have a ten-degree tilt in the upright position. If the chair has armrests, they should be short; otherwise, they get in the way.

In evaluating lighting, remember that task lighting to supplement general lighting is often essential for proper balance.

In recent years one of the biggest problems in the work environment has been the visual display terminal—the VDT, or computer screen. Glare is the major problem, causing eyestrain. An easy way to locate the cause of glare is to put a small mirror against the screen. You will see exactly where the glare is coming from so that you can either move or adjust the source or change the angle of the screen.

Nearly all computers now have detachable keyboards. Experiment with different angles and different locations for the keyboard. Moving the keyboard to a position where you can work standing may provide a welcome respite from a lengthy session of sitting.

While convenience is generally desirable, one expert believes that with respect to at least one item—the telephone—a certain amount of deliberate inconvenience is preferable. Laurence E. Morehouse says, "Your working environment should be structured not for comfort but for activity. Rather than having everything within reach, you should set yourself up so that you must move several feet to make a phone call. Ideally, the telephone should be on a shelf with a note pad alongside so that you're compelled to take all your calls standing up."[1]

As for the question of the open versus the closed office, there can be no categorical answer, but the trend of the 1970s and '80s toward more openness has been reversed. The move now is toward providing at least a modicum of privacy with the use of room dividers. Most people concentrate better and are more comfortable if they don't feel they are in a fishbowl. But too much seclusion is also a hazard, so consider the nature of the work being performed, the degree of interaction involved, and—above all—the wishes of those involved. Acceding to personal preferences with respect to more or less privacy can pay rich dividends in productivity.

Velleity

I*f you have taken* the oft-given advice to "make a list of your goals" but have found that it didn't change your life at all, it's a sure bet you've fallen victim to the most common obstacle to effective goal-setting: the Velleity Trap.

In case you're not familiar with the term, velleity means *wanting something but not wanting it badly enough to pay the price for it.* Every time you list your goals there's a temptation to include a lot of velleity: things you'd love to have if they could just be dropped in your lap; things you'd love to do if they didn't involve sacrifice. Trouble is, nothing worthwhile falls into that category.

When I ask people at a seminar to list their lifetime goals, I'm often amazed by the number of people who list as one of their goals "to write a book," but when I pin them down it becomes apparent that they have no intention whatever of sitting down in front of a typewriter for a few hundred hours. That book is no more likely to materialize than the castles in Spain they daydream about.

Or if it isn't a book, it's a language they'd like to learn. Or they want to learn to play the piano. Or they'd love to build their own boat some day and sail around the world. Or—one of the most common—they would like to own their own business.

Velleity, pure velleity.

But, you ask, aren't those legitimate goals for some people? Sure they are, but not for the ones I'm talking about. These people are quite willing to admit, when pressed, that they have made no effort toward achieving those "goals" and that there's no likelihood they ever will. They are just indulging in a flight of fantasy.

The problem is that when you realize, even at a subconscious level, that your list of "goals" includes a number of *wishes,* the list becomes worthless. It is impossible to muster the self-discipline to get started when you know that you're not looking at a list of things to work toward but a bunch of things to daydream about.

Examine your list—the one you made after reading page 38—and ask of each item, "Is this something I am really willing to pay the price for?" If not, cross it off. Then, having eliminated the velleity, you will have transformed your list into an Action Plan.

So what are you waiting for?

Voice Mail

Telephone tag is frustrating, time-consuming, and inefficient. Voice mail is one possible answer.

Voice mail is a big step up from the ordinary answering machine, which is designed for the home or a very small office. With voice mail every person in the organization with a phone has, in effect, a private answering machine that can do things an ordinary answering machine can't. It can record an incoming message and call you at a different location and play back the message. It can record a message from you that is to be delivered to a number of people and call them individually to relay the message. It can store information to be relayed at a later time only to those persons to whom you have given a special access code. It can screen and hold incoming calls and in some cases explain to the caller how many other calls are waiting. It can serve as an electronic bulletin board, available to those who need a quick verbal update on certain information.

One big disadvantage of voice mail is that since the messages must be heard instead of read, you can deal with only one at a time, and with many systems you must listen to messages sequentially instead of identifying the one you would prefer to handle first. In other words, you can't scan your voice mail.

An even more serious obstacle is that some people detest interacting with a machine instead of a person, and if your automated system is dealing with customers, as is often the case these days, you run the risk of offending them. It's tempting to carry technology too far; when it becomes a substitute for necessary one-on-one communication, it becomes a liability instead of an asset.

Voice mail isn't for everyone, but prudently used it can be a valuable tool in a busy office.

Wastebasketry

If your office is typical, roughly three-quarters of the items to be found in your files should have been placed in your wastebasket. Insufficient use of the wastebasket leads to crowded files, a chaotic desk, an overworked file clerk, and a cluttered mind.

Be ruthless in channeling paper into the wastebasket instead of into the files. Never file memos, for example, that are routine and are on file somewhere else in the organization—such things as announcements of meetings, directives that have been superseded, press releases from other departments, house newsletters, and so on. File only things that you are likely to refer to again and that are not available elsewhere.

If you find that the volume of material going into your wastebasket is large, look for ways to cut off part of the stream before it reaches your desk: Nothing could be more ridiculous than to have to read a piece of paper to determine whether you ought to be reading it at all! Perhaps your secretary can divert part of the flow directly to the wastebasket, to keep junk mail out of your "In" tray.

And ask mailers to remove your name from their list if what they are sending is of no interest to you. Even though you discard such mail without reading it, it is both time-consuming and annoying. (When the mailer fails to remove my name from a list, I've found an effective gambit: I return the envelope inscribed with the word "Deceased." It works every time.)

Weekends

Protect your weekends. Don't let work spill over into weekends except in emergencies. If God needed a rest after working six days, who are you to think you can manage without a change of pace?

A weekend of exercise and relaxation, completely removed from the cares of the office or factory, can contribute to effective use of time during the week ahead. If you can occasionally schedule a long weekend, do it.

Plan your weekends; don't just take them as they come, or you will find yourself winding up a captive of the boob tube. Having specific plans for an upcoming weekend is a morale booster for the entire preceding week and provides an incentive for getting the week's work done in time so that it won't interfere with those plans.

Wheel-Spinning

A *sure symptom* of poor time use is the mad scramble of activity that results from a poor job of goal-setting, planning, and delegating.

Working frantically in a crisis atmosphere seldom produces satisfactory results. The old maxim of the Pennsylvania Dutch, "The hurrieder I go, the behinder I get," pretty well sums up the situation.

Instead of spinning your wheels when you are faced with a crisis, take the actions that you should have taken to prevent yourself from getting there in the first place: Stop and clarify your objective, take stock of your resources, delegate whatever can be delegated, set a firm list of priorities and stick to them, try to forestall interruptions, and then start working on the item that is number one on your priority list.

After you have worked your way out of the crisis, sit down and ask yourself why it happened and what you can do to prevent its recurrence in the future.

Words to Work By

Perhaps the most valuable result of all education is the ability to make yourself do the thing you have to do when it ought to be done, whether you like it or not; it is the first lesson that ought to learned; and however early a man's training begins, it is probably the last lesson that he learns thoroughly.

—THOMAS HUXLEY

The world is cluttered up with unfinished business in the form of projects that might have been successful, if only at the tide point someone's patience had turned to active impatience.

—ROBERT UPDEGRAFF

Many of us spend half our time wishing for things we could have if we didn't spend half our time wishing.

—ALEXANDER WOOLLCOTT

Whenever you can save some of your time by offering money in its place, do so. Strangely, from their earliest beginnings men have always seemed quite happy to trade the very limited days of their lives for disks of copper, bronze, silver, and gold.

—MEYER FRIEDMAN, M.D., AND
RAY H. ROSENMAN, M.D.

It is more important to do the right thing than to do things right.

—PETER DRUCKER

The weakest creature, by concentrating his powers on a single object, can accomplish something; whereas the strongest, by dispersing his over many, may fail to accomplish anything.

—THOMAS CARLYLE

My greatest strength lies solely in my tenacity.

—LOUIS PASTEUR

Workaholic

People can become addicted to work just as they can become addicted to alcohol. Symptoms of this addiction include refusal to take a vacation, inability to put the office out of your mind on weekends, a bulging briefcase full of work, and a son or a daughter whose face is familiar, but you can't recall the name.

This syndrome can result from either of two things. The first is simply an inability to get on top of the job because of ineffective use of time (failure to establish priorities, wheel-spinning, inefficient delegation, procrastination, and so forth). In this case the techniques discussed in this book can solve the problem. The second is a subconscious *desire* to be snowed under by work and to stay that way. This may be the result of a wish to escape from an unpleasant home life, of a martyr complex, of a desire to appear indispensable, of a realization that you don't have a repertoire of leisure activities that provide satisfaction and enjoyment.*

Whatever the reason, a person in this situation clearly is concerned with *activities* (staying busy) rather than *achievements* (getting things done). Counseling can help such people cope with their problems, and it is unfortunate that so many fail to consult a psychologist or psychiatrist or psychotherapist until things reach a crisis point.

But for starters, do a bit of self-counseling. Read the section on goals and ask yourself honestly what your lifetime goals are and whether the things you are now doing are really moving you toward them. Ask yourself honestly where health stands in your list of priorities, whether the midnight oil you are burning is adversely affecting it, and whether that is an acceptable price. Ask where your family comes in your list of priorities, whether you are giving enough of yourself to your children and your spouse, and whether you are deceiving yourself by pretending that the sacrifices you are making are really for them.

Then, having accumulated a hoard of extra hours you've put into your work above and beyond the limits of reasonableness, reclaim some of that time. Plan to have lunch next Tues-

*It should be noted that working long hours does not necessarily mean you are a work addict. As a matter of fact, although a few executives work forty hours or less per week, most of the successful ones I know average considerably more than that. What differentiates them from the "workaholic" is that (1) they use their time well in achieving objectives instead of getting their kicks from the activity itself; and (2) they don't let work interfere with the really important things in life, such as friends, family, and fly fishing.

day with a personal friend instead of a business acquaintance. Plan to take Thursday afternoon off to do some out-of-the-ordinary thing, such as taking the kids to the zoo or visiting an art exhibit. You owe it to yourself.

Xenelasia

The ancient Spartans didn't care much for strangers. They had a practice called xenelasia, which meant that any magistrate could expel any stranger from the city at any time without cause. You've probably wished at times that you had something like that, some way to get rid of people who aren't welcome, who are intruding on your time. But not being a Spartan, you want to do it indirectly so as not to offend. What are your options?

First, consider how you might avoid interaction with the person in the first place. Study the physical setting of your office. Does it invite interruptions? Do you have an empty chair alongside your desk that serves as a lure to anyone who has a few minutes to kill? If so, consider getting rid of it, or make it a practice always to have a book or a file folder sitting on the chair.

Are you too close to the drinking fountain or the fax machine or the copier so that you are drawn into conversations with people who are using them? Are you too close to a busy corridor? Is your desk facing an area where people congregate? Could you get more privacy with a partition or with the judicious placement of a file cabinet or perhaps even a potted plant?

Could you preempt some of these unwelcome intrusions by not inviting the person into your office in the first place? Talk to your guest in the reception area or in the hallway.

Whenever possible, schedule a conference in the other person's office instead of in your own. When you are the "guest" instead of the "host," it's so much easier to terminate the discussion because you can just stand up and say, "I've taken enough of your time. I'll get out of here and let you get back to work." It isn't nearly so easy when you must say, in effect, "You've taken enough of my time. Please leave so that I can get back to work."

One tactful way to terminate a discussion is to summarize what has been said: "In a nutshell, Mary, as I understand it you have three basic objections to the proposal, namely . . ." Whenever you make a "summary" you are gently hinting that it's time to call a halt. Another handy ploy is, "Before I let you go, Mary, there's one more thing I'd like to mention . . ."

A wall clock placed where both you and your visitor can see it can be helpful. A glance at the clock is somehow less of an affront than looking at your wristwatch, but it accomplishes the same purpose.

Several years ago the administrative assistant to a U. S. Supreme Court justice told me of a technique he had found helpful. He would never schedule an appointment on the hour or half-hour. Instead, he would say, "Could you come by at three-twenty?" The visitor, assuming that the appointment was being sandwiched into a busy afternoon, would be less likely to prolong the visit.

I have been told that Admiral Hyman Rickover had his own twist to the xenelasia idea. Annoyed by people who were overstaying their welcome, he had someone saw an inch off the front two legs of the wooden chair he used for guests. He maintained it kept visits much shorter.

All of these indirect techniques have their place, but often your best bet is a blunt statement: "Jim, I wish I could give you more time, but there are some other things I must get to right away." That may ruffle a few feathers, but don't let that bother you. Be a Spartan!

Yesterday Trap

When *Charles M. Schwab*, one of the great tycoons of the past century, was a very young man he worked for Andrew Carnegie. It was Carnegie, he later said, who taught him one of the most important lessons of life: the need to avoid the Yesterday Trap.

One day while checking the previous day's production for the steel plant he managed, Schwab was elated to note that a new record had been set. He fired off a telegram to Carnegie: "All records broken yesterday," and gave him the figures. Instead of congratulations he received in reply a five-word telegram that said simply, "What have you done today?"

If resting on yesterday's laurels was futile a century ago, it is even more so today. As someone has said, "The future is hurtling toward us with the speed of an express train." New technical developments such as the fax machine, the cellular phone, the laptop computer, the VCR, voice mail, and so forth, change almost overnight the way people do things, and the successful people and organizations are those that are flexible enough to adjust quickly—which means forgetting about the achievements and problems of the past and focusing time and attention on the unprecedented problems and opportunities of the present.

It isn't easy to put yesterday behind us because the past is so much easier to work with than the future. Many people take comfort in the fact that the past can be reduced to numbers, charts, and graphs; they are uncomfortable with the ambiguity, uncertainty, and risk involved in the future, so they spend too much time recording and analyzing what has happened and not enough on what should happen now.

In avoiding the Yesterday Trap it is especially important not to spend precious time regretting mistakes you may have made. A famous New York psychiatrist, nearing the end of a long and illustrious career several years ago, said that the most useful concept he had discovered for helping people turn their lives around was what he called his "four little words." The first two were *if only.* "Many of my patients have spent their lives living in the past," he said, "anguishing about what they should have done in various situations. 'If only I had prepared better for that interview . . .' 'If only I had expressed my true feelings to the boss . . .' 'If only I had taken that accounting course . . .' "

Wallowing in this sea of regret is a serious emotional drain. The antidote is simple: Eliminate those two words from your vocabulary. Substitute the words *next time* and tell yourself, "Next time I'm going to be prepared . . . Next time I'm going to speak out . . . Next time I'm going to take that class . . ."

Practice this simple technique until it becomes a habit. Never rehash errors you've made. When you find yourself doing so, simply tell yourself, "Next time I'll do it differently." You'll find this closes the door on the matter, freeing you to devote your time and your thoughts to the present and the future instead of the past.

A FINAL WORD

Above all else, good time management involves an awareness that today is all we ever have to work with. The past is irretrievably gone, the future is only a concept. Everything that is accomplished in the world is the result of someone's realization that today is the only time we can really control.

If that seems rather elementary to you, be assured that the vast majority of your fellow human beings seldom fully grasp that self-evident truth.

Thomas Carlyle put it this way: "Our main task is not to see what lies dimly perceived in the future but to do the thing which lies immediately at hand." John Ruskin had the word TODAY carved into a small marble block that he kept on his desk as a constant reminder to "Do It Now."

But my favorite quotation is this one by an anonymous philosopher:

> YESTERDAY is a cancelled check. Forget it.
> TOMORROW is a promissory note. Don't count on it.
> TODAY is ready cash. Use it!

NOTES

Behavior Modification
1. As quoted in *The Pryor Report*, November 1986.

Cellular Phone
1. Quoted in *A Commonplace Book*, Sherwood Grover and James D. Hammond editors (Aptos, California: Grace Hoper Press, 1969), p. 26.

Exercise: The Time Factor
1. *Newsweek*, November 13, 1989, p. 77.

Indecision: The Paralysis of Analysis
1. Quoted in William J. Knaus, *Do It Now* (Englewood Cliffs, N.J.: Prentice-Hall, 1979), p. 52.
2. James Calano and Jeff Salzman, *CareerTracking* (New York: Simon & Schuster, 1988), p. 104.

Information Overload
1. Quoted in Robert W. Glasgow, "Aristocrats Have Always Been Bitches," *Psychology Today* (January 1973), p. 63.

Laziness
1. Edwin C. Bliss, *Doing It Now: A 12-Step Program for Curing Procrastination and Achieving Your Goals* (New York: Charles Scribner's Sons, 1983).
2. William Bernbach, *Bill Bernbach Said . . .*, booklet published by DDB Needham Worldwide, 437 Madison Avenue, New York, N.Y. 10022.

MBO: A Reappraisal
1. Tom Peters, *Thriving on Chaos* (New York: Alfred A. Knopf, 1987), p. 603.

2. Laurence J. Peter, *The Peter Prescription* (New York: Bantam Books, 1972), p. 145.

Meetings: Before
1. Nathan Edelson, "Business Meetings on the Run," *Wall Street Journal,* March 13, 1989, p. A-3.
2. Ibid.

Meetings: After
1. Joseph D. Cooper, *How to Get More Done in Less Time* (Garden City, N.Y.: Doubleday & Co., 1971), p. 289.

Meetings: Stimulating Input
1. *Boardroom Reports,* April 15, 1990, p. 9.

Meetings: The When
1. Jeffrey J. Mayer, *If You Haven't Got Time to Do It Right, When Will You Have Time to Do It Over?* (New York: Simon & Schuster, 1990), p. 96.

Meetings: Formal
1. Quoted in *The Standard Code of Parliamentary Procedure,* Third Edition (New York: McGraw-Hill, 1988), p. 237.

Paperwork: The Marks & Spencer Experience
1. Goronwy Rees, *St. Michael, A History of Marks & Spencer* (London: Pan Books Ltd., 1973), p. 232.

Perfectionism
1. Gail Sheehy, *Passages* (New York: E. P. Dutton, 1976), p. 513.

Quiet Time
1. Merrill E. Douglass and Donna N. Douglass, *Manage Your Time, Manage Your Work, Manage Yourself,* (New York: Amacom, 1980), p. 111.
2. Northwestern Mutual Life Insurance Company, Milwaukee, Wisconsin, *The Power of Quiet,* 1988.

Radical Surgery
1. Robert Townsend, *Up the Organization* (New York: Fawcett World Library, 1978), p. 75.
2. Peter Drucker, *The Effective Executive* (New York: Harper & Row, 1967), p. 109.

Sleep
1. *The Sleep Better, Live Better Guide* (pamphlet), p. 1, published by Better Sleep Council, P.O. Box 13, Washington, D.C. 20044.
2. Ibid., p. 2.

Speed Reading
1. James T. McCay, *The Management of Time* (Englewood Cliffs, N.J.: Prentice-Hall, 1959), p. 142.

Stand-up Desk
1. "Proceedings of the Human Factors Society Los Angeles Symposium," November 1989, University of Southern California.

Technophobia
1. *1988 Inc. Office Guide* (Boston: Inc. Publishing Co., 1988), p. 76.
2. Stephen D. Solomon, "Use Technology to Manage People," *Inc.*, May 1990, p. 124.

Tempo
1. Charles H. Ford, *How to Overcome Business Frustrations* (published by *Nation's Business*, Washington, D.C., 1975), p. 14.

Time Management and Your Heart
1. Interview with the author.
2. *Boardroom Reports*, May 15, 1990, p. 14.

Upward Delegation
1. William Oncken, Jr., and Donald L. Wass, "Management Time: Who's Got the Monkey?" *Harvard Business Review* (November–December 1974), p. 76.

User-Friendly Office
1. Laurence E. Morehouse and Leonard Gross, *Maximum Performance* (New York: Simon & Schuster, 1977), p. 76.

NOTES

NOTES

NOTES

NOTES

KNOW YOUR CHILD'S I.Q.
Glenn Wilson and Diana Grylls

The simple way to test your child's I.Q. . . . and improve his ratings.

I.Q. is by no means the be all and end all of a child's existence, as the authors make clear in this fascinating book, but it is a useful rough and ready guide to the performance he *should* achieve in his studies, and a very useful yardstick for anxious parents.

Following the simple, thoroughly tested methods outlined, parents can arrive at an accurate profile of their child's abilities and teach him to improve his performance in tests given at school.

0 7088 0982 0
FUTURA PUBLICATIONS
SELF HELP

IMPROVE YOUR I.Q.
Glenn Wilson

HOW INTELLIGENT ARE YOU?

Most people regard I.Q. tests in the same light as crossword puzzles. You are either born with the knack of doing them, or you are not, and therefore the level of your intelligence remains static.

But Glenn Wilson, Doctor of Psychology at the London Institute of Psychiatry, believes that it is actually possible to improve one's I.Q. by constant practice of tests ranging from word puzzles to simple mathematical problems.

0 8600 7026 3
GENERAL NON FICTION

DON'T SAY YES WHEN YOU WANT TO SAY NO

Herbert Fensterheim Ph.D.
and Jean Baer

Are you the kind of person who endures a cold bowl of soup rather than complain to the waiter?

Do you dread returning something to a shop even if there's a good reason to do so? If someone talks loudly during a movie, can you ask him to be quiet?

Don't Say Yes When You Want To Say No will teach you how to assert your rights in work, in marriage, in sex, in social situations and family life. It will help you train yourself to recognize your own fundamental human worth and make others recognize it too.

Don't Say Yes When You Want To Say No will show you that self-assertiveness means being able to say "no" when you want to, and knowing how to express anger and resentment when you have to. It means being successful and not feeling guilty about it. This life-changing programme is easier than you think!

0 8600 7437 4
FUTURA/NON FICTION

MAKING LIFE RIGHT WHEN IT FEELS ALL WRONG

*Herbert Fensterheim Ph.D.
and Jean Baer*

Do you feel let down and exploited by your friends?
Unappreciated at work? Misunderstood by your partner?
Dissatisfied with yourself? The time has come to stop being
a victim and start taking control of your life.

With a refreshing blend of humour and realism, *Making Life
Right* reveals how you can come out on top. Using
psychological techniques and down-to-earth commonsense,
it shows how to achieve job satisfaction, fulfilling friendships
and a rewarding sex life. Recognize your worth, accept your
limitations and develop the confidence to conquer your weak
spots – you *can* make your life right!

0 7088 4209 7
FUTURA PUBLICATIONS
NON FICTION

GO FOR IT!
Dr Irene C. Kassorla

What do *you* consider to be winning? Success in your career, sporting or artistic achievements? Or richly enjoyable relationships with your loved ones? Whatever your personal dreams, it really is possible to transform them into reality. Everyone has the power within them to:

- ► learn positively from initial failures
- ► alter their life for the better
- ► transform losing patterns into winning skills
- ► increase vital feelings of self-esteem

GO FOR IT!

Happiness and success are contagious – now you can make them happen to you.

Experience the joy of winning as you reach out for your goals!

0 7088 2750 0
FUTURA PUBLICATIONS
NON FICTION

WIDOWS

The explosive truth behind 25 years of Western intelligence disasters

William R. Corson
Susan B. Trento
Joseph J. Trento

For 25 years a series of secret battles was fought by American counter-intelligence experts against the intelligence services of the Soviet Union. The Russians won. Unprecedented in scope, *Widows* uncovers the reasons behind these repeated Soviet victories.

For the first time, members of America's intelligence community speak out about four interlinked major intelligence disasters. *Widows* reveals:

* the identity of the first Soviet mole in the CIA.
* the implications of the real story of John Arthur Paisley, a key CIA officer who disappeared in 1978.
* the truth concerning Nikolay Fedorovich Artamonov who defected in 1959, gained access to the core of American intelligence and disappeared 15 years later in Vienna.
* the harrowing tale of Ralph Joseph Sigler, the FBI and army intelligence premier double agent who was found electrocuted in a motel room. *Widows* explains how Sigler really died – and why.

A full portrait of the behind-the-scenes conflicts that derailed much of Western intelligence, this is a fascinating and disturbing book.

'A hot property . . . a masterful job of investigative journalism' *Sunday Telegraph*

0 7088 4546 0
FUTURA PUBLICATIONS
NON FICTION

Futura now offers an exciting range of quality titles by both established and new authors. All of the books in this series are available from:
Sphere Books,
Cash Sales Department,
P.O. Box 11,
Falmouth,
Cornwall TR10 9EN.

Alternatively you may fax your order to the above address. Fax No. 0326 376423.

Payments can be made as follows: Cheque, postal order (payable to Macdonald & Co (Publishers) Ltd) or by credit cards, Visa/Access. Do not send cash or currency. UK customers and B.F.P.O.: please send a cheque or postal order (no currency) and allow £1.00 for postage and packing for the first book, plus 50p for the second book, plus 30p for each additional book up to a maximum charge of £3.00 (7 books plus).

Overseas customers including Ireland, please allow £2.00 for postage and packing for the first book, plus £1.00 for the second book, plus 50p for each additional book.

NAME (Block Letters) ....

ADDRESS ....

....

☐ I enclose my remittance for _____

☐ I wish to pay by Access/Visa Card

Number ☐☐☐☐☐☐☐☐☐☐☐☐☐☐☐☐

Card Expiry Date ☐☐☐☐